JAQUELINE MITCHELL
is a writer and a compiler of anthologies,
specializing in social and cultural history,
and an editor of non-fiction.

ERIC FITCH DAGLISH (1892–1966)
was a wood engraver and illustrator.
His book *Woodcuts of British Birds*
was published in 1925.

BIRDS
An Anthology

COMPILED BY
JAQUELINE MITCHELL

Woodcuts by Eric Fitch Daglish

Bodleian Library
UNIVERSITY OF OXFORD

For Joy Mitchell (1912–2012),
who first introduced me to watching birds, and for my parents,
Dnys Mitchell (1919–1986) and Christine Mitchell (1918–2019),
who encouraged it

First published in 2020 by the Bodleian Library
Broad Street, Oxford OX1 3BG
www.bodleianshop.co.uk
ISBN 978 1 85124 529 1

Introduction and selection © Jaqueline Mitchell, 2020
Photography © Bodleian Library, University of Oxford, 2020

Illustrations are reproduced by kind permission of the Daglish family
and taken from the following books by Eric Fitch Daglish:
Woodcuts of British Birds (E. Benn, 1925),
Oxford, Bodleian Library, 17156 d.87
The Smaller Birds and *The Larger Birds* (J.M. Dent, 1928)
Oxford, Bodleian Library, Opie FF 219 and Opie FF 215

Every effort has been made to trace copyright holders and to obtain
permission for the use of copyright material (see also p. 264); any errors or
omissions will be corrected in future editions of the book.

Cover design by Dot Little at the Bodleian Library
Designed and typeset in 12 on 14 Perpetua by illuminati, Grosmont
Printed and bound in China by C&C Offset Printing Co. Ltd
on 120 gsm Baijin FSC woodfree

British Library Catalogue in Publishing Data
A CIP record of this publication is available from the British Library

CONTENTS

INTRODUCTION

LAST NIGHT AS I WALKED HOME, I saw my first swifts of the season. Wheeling high, high overhead, darting after insects on the wing, returned from their winter grounds far south in Africa, they are as familiar now in the village in May as the cuckoo. And each year they sign to us that spring has finally arrived. From the back of my house some nights, more frequently than not, I hear owls hooting; there are goldfinches in the garden, sometimes a wren or a woodpecker, more often blue tits or long-tailed tits. As I garden, robins and blackbirds watch from inches away, ready to pounce on whatever morsel I unearth as I dig. Today, as in my childhood, I am pleased to inhabit a bird-filled world. Back then, I watched adults observe and photograph birds, spent summer dawns watching swallows sweep over the hayfields, and once went hawking with an artist friend of my aunt. This book was influenced by those early years, which spurred a continuing interest in birds and bird behaviour.

I have long wanted to 'do something' on birds; finding that anthologies largely focused on poetry, I felt that a new book that especially drew on archival material and the long history of birdwatching might be welcome. In early conversations with Bodleian Library Publishing, we decided to focus on historical rather than contemporary material, hoping to show the rich heritage of prose on birds and birdwatching. While this book does contain some contemporary material – one could hardly omit Ted Hughes, or J.A. Baker on the peregrine, and Barbara Kingsolver's descriptions of a dawn chorus in her novel *Prodigal Summer* clearly derive from her own enthusiasm for natural history – mostly readers will find pieces from the eleventh century to the mid-twentieth. The earliest pieces are from Roman times, the latest those of our own time.

I also wanted this book to represent writers from around the world, though writing in English. And so there are pieces from Evliya Çelebi, who in his Ottoman explorations of the Nile in the seventeenth century describes a mountain of birds where 'several hundred thousand birds of various kinds' have flown there from Turkey. We can read of cranes dancing in India; of hawking in the Arabian desert; of the great conservationist President Theodore Roosevelt's travels in Brazil.

Readers will undoubtedly find some of their own favourites missing: inevitably, my choices will not always be theirs. But my hope is that, alongside old familiars, readers will discover old writings anew or passages never previously encountered. I am grateful too that the Estate of Eric Fitch Daglish allowed us to use his fine etchings: his graceful work deserves, I think, to be better known.

Today, we live in a time of crisis in the natural world; where habitats that many believed a constant are challenged by climate change. With the increase in desertification and reduction in breeding grounds, bird life is threatened, alongside our own. Nearly sixty years ago Rachel Carson warned us of a *Silent Spring*. One of the things that this book reveals is that much further back, and for far too long, the negative impact of human expansion on our natural world has been noted; and yet we have done little to remedy this. One can only hope that now it is widely acknowledged that we are at a critical tipping point, we will at last heed the drift downwards of wildlife and finally resolve not to prioritize our own needs above those of all other species.

In 1933, the Welsh writer W.H. Davies wrote in *My Birds* that 'to sit in one's own garden and listen to the Blackbird's song ... seems to be life at its highest value, to which all other kinds of life appear dull, unhealthy, and wasteful.' Back in 1896 (in his *Handbook of Birds of Eastern North America*), Frank M. Chapman told readers that they should study birds, as being 'possessed of such unusual interest', in 'origin and relationships, their distribution in time and space, their migrations, their nesting habits, their form and color, and all the details of their structure and life' that 'birds, more than any other animals, may serve as bonds between man and Nature'. And in 2019, in his newly published (and rather wonderful) book *Something of His Art: Walking to Lubeck with J.S. Bach*, Horatio Clare notes, as he traces Bach's journey from Arnstadt through the woods of southern Germany, a continuum in the soundscape of birdsong over three centuries. In this book, I hope readers will find in narratives recorded over a thousand years wordscapes to accompany their own observational journeys.

Jaqueline Mitchell

AUTHOR'S NOTE Each chapter is arranged in date-of-birth order. All titles for prose extracts are my own.

WHAT IS A BIRD?
Definitions over time

ARISTOTLE (384–322 BCE)
Creatures that have feathered wings are classed as a genus
under the name of *bird* ... The bird is remarkable among
animals as having two feet, like man; only, by the way, it
bends them backwards as quadrupeds bend their hind legs,
as was noticed previously. It has neither hands nor front
feet, but wings – an exceptional structure as compared
with other animals...

from *The History of Animals* (*c.* 350 BCE)

PLINY THE ELDER (*C.* 23–79 CE)
The first distinctive characteristic among birds is that
which bears reference more especially to their feet: they
have either hooked talons, or else toes, or else, again, they
belong to the web-footed class, geese for instance, and
most of the aquatic birds. Those which have hooked talons
feed, for the most part, upon nothing but flesh.

from *Natural History* (77 CE)

Eᴘʜʀᴀɪᴍ Cʜᴀᴍʙᴇʀs (c. 1680–1740)

Bɪʀᴅ, a two-footed animal, covered with feathers, and furnished with wings, whereby it can sustain itself in the air, and fly from place to place.

Birds are usually divided into *terrestrial* and *aquatic*.

Terrestrial Bɪʀᴅs are subdivided into those which have *crooked beaks* and *talons*; and those whose beaks and claws are *streighter*.

Of birds with *crooked beaks and talons*, some are carnivorous and rapacious, called *birds of prey*; others frugivorous, called by the general name of *parrots*. ...

Aquatic Bɪʀᴅs, or *water-fowl*, are distinguished into such as *walk* in the waters, and such as *swim* in them.

Aquatics which *walk* are all cloven-footed, and generally have long legs, and those naked, or bare of feathers, a good way above the knee, that they may the more conveniently wade in waters. ... Of aquatics, which *swim* in the water, some are *fissipedes*, cloven-footed, as the moor-hen and coot, &c. but most are whole-footed, or web-footed, *palmipedes*.

from *Cyclopaedia: or An Universal Dictionary of Arts and Sciences* (1741)

Cᴀʀʟ Lɪɴɴᴀᴇᴜs (1707–1778)

Bɪʀᴅs: *Lungs* respire alternately; *jaws* incumbent, naked, extended, without teeth; *eggs* covered with a calcareous shell; *organs* of sense, tongue, nostrils, eyes and ears without auricles; *covering*, incumbent, imbricate feathers;

supporters, feet 2, wings 2; and a heart-shaped rump;
fly in the *air*, and *sing*.

from *A General System of Nature, through the Three Grand
Kingdoms of Animals, Vegetables, and Minerals, Systematically
Divided into their Several Classes, Orders, Genera, Species,
and Varieties, with their Habitations,Manners, Economy,
Structure and Peculiarities* (1735; *trans.* 1802–06)

SAMUEL JOHNSON (1709–1784)
BIRD. *n.s.* [bɪŋð, or bŋɪð, a chicken, Saxon.] A general
term for the feathered kind; a fowl.

from *Dictionary of the English Language* (1755)

REVD J.G. WOODS (1827–1889)
The most conspicuous external characteristic by which
the BIRDS are distinguished from all other inhabitants of
earth, is the feathery robe which invests their bodies, and
which serves the double purpose of clothing and progression. For the first of these two objects it is admirably
adapted, as the long, slender filaments of the feathers are
not only in themselves indifferent conductors of heat, but
entangle among their multitudinous fibres a considerable
amount of air, which resists the ingress or the egress of
external or internal heat, and thus preserves the bird in a
moderate temperature through the icy blasts of winter or
the burning rays of the summer sun. A similar function is
discharged by the furry coats of many mammalia; but the
feathers serve another office, which is not possessed by hair
or fur. They aid the creature in progression, and enable it
to raise and to sustain itself in the atmosphere.

from *The Illustrated Natural History: Birds* (1859)

Bird, n.

1. a. *orig.* The general name for the young of the feathered tribes; a young bird; a chicken, eaglet, etc.; a nestling. The only sense in Old English; found in literature down to 1600; still retained in northern dialect as 'a hen and her birds'.

2. Any feathered vertebrate animal: a member of the second class (*Aves*) of the great Vertebrate group, the species of which are most nearly allied to the Reptiles, but distinguished by their warm blood, feathers, and adaptation of the fore limbs as wings, with which most species fly in the air.

Oxford English Dictionary (1887; 2019 online edn)

A BIRDING YEAR
Spring

from *The Owl*

MICHAEL DRAYTON (1563–1631)

I on a suddaine drop't into a trance:
Wherein me thought some God or power devine
Did my cleere knowledge wondrously refine.
For that amongst those sundry varying notes,
Which the Birds sent from their Melodious throats,
Each Silvan sound I truely understood,
Become a perfect Linguist of the Wood:
Their flight, their song, and every other signe,
By which the World did anciently devine:
As the old Tuskans in that skill profound,
Which first great Car, and wise Tyresias found,
To me bequeath'd their knowledge to discry,
The depth and secrets of their Augurie.
One I could heare appointing with his sweeting
A place convenient for their secret meeting.
Others, when Winter shortly should declyne,
How they would couple at Saint Valentine.
Some other Birds that of their Loves forsaken,
To the close deserts had themselves betaken,
And in the darke Groaves where they made aboad,
Sang many a sad and mournfull Palinod.
And every Bird shew'd in his proper kinde,
What vertue, nature had to him assign'de.
The pretty Turtle, and the kissing Dove,
Their faiths in Wedlock, and chast nuptiall Love:
The Hens to Women sanctitie expresse,
Hallowing their Egges: the Swallow clenlinesse,
Sweetning her nest, and purging it of dong

And every howr is picking of her yong.
The Herne by soaring shewes tempestuous showers,
The Princely Cocke distinguisheth the howres.
The Kyte, his traine him guiding in the aire,
Prescribes the helme, instructing how to stere.
The Crane to labour, fearing some rough flawe,
With sand and gravell burthening his craw.
Noted by man, which by the same did finde
To ballast Shippes for steddines in winde.
And by the forme and order in his flight,
To march in warre, and how to watch by night.
The first of house that ere did groundsell lay,
Which then was homely of rude lome and clay;
Learn'd of the Martin, Philomel in spring,
Teaching by art her little one to sing;
By whose cleere voyce sweet musicke first was found,
Before Amphyon ever knew a sound.
Covering with Mosse the deads unclosed eye:
The little Red-breast teacheth charytie.
So many there in sundry things excell,
Time scarse could serve their properties to tell.

The Mountain of Birds

Evliya Çelebi (1611–1682)

The tongue falls short at describing this great mountain.
Every year in the spring several hundred thousand birds of
various kinds – but mainly storks and goldfinches – come
from the direction of Turkey and settle on this mountain.
The mountain plains swarm with them, so that one can
hardly find a place to set one's foot, and their cries are
loud enough to make one's gall bladder burst. The people
of the region are aware of the spectacle and come to view
it from a distance, but no one can seize any of the birds or
throw stones at them. On top of the mountain, on a sandy
plain, is a cemetery. Each sarcophagus contains thousands
of birds of various sorts – but mainly storks – buried in
their shrouds (i.e. mummified). The (living) birds all come
to visit this cemetery, circling above it and squawking and
lamenting. Then they land in the mountain plains. Most
of the buried birds are visible outside the graveyard. Their
bodies and feathers are fresh and have not decayed inside
their shrouds, which are made of date-palm fibres. No
one knows the reason why these birds are buried here in
their shrouds, nor have I seen it mentioned in any of the
histories. This humble one actually brought two of these
mummified birds to Ketkhuda Ibrahim Pasha so he could
see them.

from *The Book of Travels* (*Seyâhatnâme*)

Ode to the Cuckoo

MARK AKENSIDE (1721–1770)

O Rustick herald of the spring!
   At length in yonder woody vale
Fast by the brook I hear thee sing;
   And studious of thy homely tale
Amid the vespers of the grove,
Amid the chanting choir of love,
   Thy sage responses hail.

The time has been when I have frown'd
   To hear thy voice the woods invade;
And while thy solemn accent drown'd
   Some sweeter poet of the shade
Thus thought I, thus the sons of Care
Some constant youth or gen'rous fair
   With dull advice upbraid.

I said 'While Philomela's song
   Proclaims the passion of the grove
It ill beseems a cuckoo's tongue
   Her charming language to reprove.'
Alas! how much a lover's ear
Hates all the sober truth to hear,
   The sober truth of love!

When hearts are in each other blest,
   When nought but lofty faith can rule
The nymph's and swain's consenting breast,
   How cuckoolike in Cupid's school

With store of grave prudential saws
On Fortune's pow'r and Custom's laws
   Appears each friendly fool!

Yet think betimes, ye gentle Train!
   Whom love, and hope, and fancy, sway,
Who ev'ry harsher care disdain,
   Who by the morning judge the day,
Think that in April's fairest hours
To warbling shades and painted flow'rs
   The Cuckoo joins his lay.

The Opening of the Birch Leaves

WILLIAM COBBETT (1763–1835)

The opening of the birch leaves is the signal for the pheasant
to begin to crow, for the blackbird to whistle, and the
thrush to sing; and, just when the oak-buds begin to look
reddish, and not a day before, the whole tribe of finches
burst forth in songs from every bough, while the lark,
imitating them all, carries the joyous sounds to the sky.

from *Rural Rides* (1830)

The Young Bullfinches

DOROTHY WORDSWORTH (1771–1855)

Friday, 28th [May 1802].— … We sate in the orchard. The
sky cloudy, the air sweet and cool. The young bullfinches,
in their party-coloured raiment, bustle about among
the blossoms, and poise themselves like wire-dancers or
tumblers, shaking the twigs and dashing off the blossoms.

from *Journals of Dorothy Wordsworth*

The Banquet

JAMES JENNINGS OF HUNTSPILL (1772–1833)

Behold now the banquet! And, first, we remark,
That the *banqueting-hall* was a large shady park;
The table a glade – cloth a carpet of green,
Where sweet-smelling shrubs strew'd about might be seen.
The lilac put forth her delights in the vale;
Other spring-flowers' odours were mix'd with the gale.
With encouraging smile nature sat at the feast;
Her converse a charm that enraptured each guest.
The viands were various to suit every taste,
Got together by *magic*, assisted by *haste*:
The dishes, all simple, no surfeit produce;
Nor did wine's effervescence excite to abuse.
There was CORN – *wheat*, *oats*, *barley*, for many a FOWL;
There was *grass* for the GOOSE, and a *mouse* for the OWL.
There were *pease* for the ROOK, as an elegant treat;
For the CROW there was *carrion*, he glories to eat.
The BULFINCH's feast was some buds from the plum,

That, torn fresh from the tree, made the gardener look
  glum.
For PHEASANTS and NIGHTINGALES, *ants' eggs* were found;
And *flies* for the SWALLOWS in numbers abound.
For the SEA-GULL was many a *cock-chafer grub*;
Many WARBLERS pick'd *worms* from the tree or the shrub;
The SEA-BIRDS directed attention to *fish*;
The DUCK partook of almost every dish.
For the SWAN were some *water-plants* pluck'd from the
  pond;
Of *fish* the KING-FISHERS evinc'd they were fond.
The DIVERS, GREBES, GUILLEMOTS, WATER-RAILS, too,
On the dishes of *fish* all instinctively flew.
For the GOLDFINCH was *groundsel*, a delicate bit;
There was *sunflower-seed* for the saucy TOMTIT.
For the CRANE was an *eel*; for the THRUSH was a *snail*;
And *barley* for PARTRIDGE, for PIGEON, and QUAIL.
For the CUCKOO, an *earthworm* – his greatest delight;
Some HAWKS, of *fowl*, *flesh*, or *fish*, seiz'd what they might;
But the KESTRIL, a *mouse* to all dainties preferr'd;
While the SHRIKE pounc'd, at once, on some poor helpless
  bird.
For the HOUSE-SPARROW, *wheat* – he's reputed a thief;
The EAGLE himself got a slice of *raw beef*.
The TURKEY of *apples* partook as a treat,
And the COCK and the HEN caught up a *bone of cold meat*.
The DESSERT? – It consisted of only *one* thing:
A clear stream of water just fresh from the spring.

from *Ornithologia, or The Birds* (1828)

The Skylark

WILLIAM YARRELL (1784–1856)

The Skylark is so abundant, so well known and so universal
a favourite, as to require little more than a general reference
here to the points of greatest interest in its history. It is
an inhabitant of all the countries of Europe, preferring
cultivated districts, and particularly arable land. Here in
early spring its cheerful and exhilarating song, fresh as the
season, is the admiration of all. The bird rises on quivering
wing, almost perpendicularly, singing as he flies, and, even
after gaining an extraordinary elevation, so powerful is his
voice, that his wild, joyous notes may be heard distinctly
when the pained eye can trace his course no longer, but an
ear well tuned to his song can yet determine by the notes
whether he is still ascending, stationary or on the descent,
for the strain is continued on his downward course till
he approaches the ground, when it stops abruptly, and
with a headlong dart the bird alights. The appearance of a
Merlin also will cause the sudden cessation of the song – at
whatever height the performer may be, his wings are closed
and he drops to the earth like a falling stone; the Kestrel,
however, is treated with indifference, and in the presence
of a Sparrow-Hawk the Skylark knows that safety is to be
sought aloft. Occasionally he sings when standing near his
mate, or more rarely when perched on a bush; but his most
lively strains are poured forth during flight, and even in
confinement this 'scorner of the ground' tramples his turf
and flutters his wings while singing, as if muscular motion
was with him a necessary accompaniment to his music.

from *A History of British Birds* (1843)

Chuck Will's Widow

John James Audubon (1785–1851)

About the middle of March, the forests of Louisiana are
heard to echo with the well-known notes of this interesting
bird. No sooner has the sun disappeared, and the nocturnal
insects emerge from their burrows, than the sounds,
'*chuck-will's-widow*', repeated with great clearness and power
six or seven times in as many seconds, strike the ear of
every individual, bringing to the mind a pleasure mingled
with a certain degree of melancholy, which I have often
found very soothing. The sounds of the Goatsucker, at
all events, forebode a peaceful and calm night, and I have
more than once thought, are conducive to lull the listener
to repose.

The deep ravines, shady swamps, and extensive pine
ridges, are all equally resorted to by these birds; for in all
such places they find ample means of providing for their
safety during the day, and of procuring food under night.
Their notes are seldom heard in cloudy weather, and never
when it rains. Their roosting places are principally the
hollows of decayed trees, whether standing or prostrate,
from which latter they are seldom raised during the day,
excepting while incubation is in progress. In these hollows
I have found them, lodged in the company of several
species of bats, the birds asleep on the mouldering particles
of the wood, the bats clinging to the sides of the cavities.
When surprised in such situations, instead of trying to
effect their escape by flying out, they retire backwards to
the farthest corners, ruffle all the feathers of their body,
open their mouth to its full extent, and utter a hissing kind

of murmur, not unlike that of some snakes. When seized
and brought to the light of day, they open and close their
eyes in rapid succession, as if it were painful for them to
encounter so bright a light. They snap their little bill in the
manner of Fly-catchers, and shuffle along as if extremely
desirous of making their escape.

    … At the approach of night, this bird begins to sing
clearly and loudly, and continues its notes for about a
quarter of an hour. At this time it is perched on a fence-
stake, or on the decayed branch of a tree in the interior
of the woods, seldom on the ground. The sounds or notes
which it emits seem to cause it some trouble, as it raises
and lowers its head in quick succession at each of them.
This over, the bird launches into the air, and is seen
sweeping over the cotton fields or the sugar plantations,
cutting all sorts of figures, mounting, descending, or
sailing, with so much ease and grace, that one might be
induced to call it the *Fairy of the night*.

from *Birds of America* (1827–38)

Thrushes Singing into Spring
JOHN KEATS (1795–1821)

Letter XXXVIII. – To George and Thomas Keats
Hampstead, Saturday [21 February 1818]
… The Thrushes and Blackbirds have been singing me
into an idea that it was Spring, and almost that leaves were
on the trees. So that black clouds and boisterous winds
seem to have mustered and collected in full Divan, for
the purpose of convincing me to the contrary. Taylor says

my poem shall be out in a month, I think he will be out before it....

The thrushes are singing now as if they would speak to the winds, because their big brother Jack, the Spring, was not far off.

An English Cuckoo in India
EMILY EDEN (1797–1869)

April 29, 1838.
There never was such delicious weather, just like Mr. Wodehouse's gruel, 'cool, but not too cool'; and there is an English cuckoo talking English – at least, he is trying, but he evidently left England as a cadet, with his education incomplete, for he cannot get further than *cuck* – and there is a blackbird singing. ... It certainly is very pleasant to be in a pretty place, with a nice climate. Not that I would not set off this instant, and go *dâk* all over the hot plains, and through the hot wind, if I were told I might sail home the instant I arrived at Calcutta; but as nobody makes me that offer, I can wait here better than anywhere else – like meat, we *keep* better here.

from *Up the Country: Letters Written to Her Sister from the Upper Provinces of India*

The First Cuckoo

EDWARD JENNER (1822–1896)

The first appearance of Cuckoos in Gloucestershire (the part of England where these observations were made) is about the 17th of April. The song of the male, which is well known, soon proclaims its arrival. The song of the female (if the peculiar notes of which it is composed may be so called) is widely different, and has been so little attended to, that I believe few are acquainted with it. I know not how to convey to you a proper idea of it by a comparison with the notes of any other bird; but the cry of the Dab-chick bears the nearest resemblance to it.

Unlike the generality of birds, Cuckoos do not pair. When a female appears on the wing, she is often attended by two or three males, who seem to be earnestly contending for her favours. From the time of her appearance, till after the middle of summer, the nests of the birds selected to receive her egg are to be found in great abundance; but, like the other migrating birds, she does not begin to lay till some weeks after her arrival. I never could procure an egg till after the middle of May, though probably an early-coming Cuckoo may produce one sooner.

The Cuckoo makes choice of the nests of a great variety of small birds. I have known its egg intrusted to the care of the Hedge-sparrow, the Water-wagtail, the Titlark, the Yellow-hammer, the green Linnet, and the Whinchat. Among these it generally selects the three former; but shews a much greater partiality to the Hedge-sparrow than to any of the rest: therefore, for the purpose of avoiding confusion, this bird only, in the following account, will be considered as the foster-parent of the Cuckoo, except in instances which are particularly specified.

The Hedge-sparrow commonly takes up four or five days in laying her eggs. During this time (generally after she has laid one or two) the Cuckoo contrives to deposit her egg among the rest, leaving the future care of it entirely to the Hedge-sparrow. This intrusion often occasions some discomposure; for the old Hedge-sparrow at intervals, whilst she is sitting, not unfrequently throws out some of her own eggs, and sometimes injures them in such a way that they become addle; so that it more frequently happens, that only two or three Hedge-sparrow's eggs are hatched with the Cuckoo's than otherwise: but whether this be the case or not, she sits the same length of time as if no foreign egg had been introduced, the Cuckoo's egg requiring no longer incubation than her own. ...

When the Hedge-sparrow has sat her usual time, and disengaged the young Cuckoo and some of her own offspring from the shell, her own young ones, and any of her eggs that remain unhatched, are soon turned out, the young Cuckoo remaining possessor of the nest, and sole object of her future care. The young birds are not previously killed, nor are the eggs demolished; but all are left to perish together, either entangled about the bush which contains the nest, or lying on the ground under it. ...

There seems to be no precise time fixed for the departure of young Cuckoos. I believe they go off in succession, probably as soon as they are capable of taking care of themselves; for although they stay here till they become nearly equal in size and growth of plumage to the old Cuckoo, yet in this very state the fostering care of the Hedge-sparrow is not withdrawn from them. I have frequently seen the young Cuckoo of such a size that the Hedge-sparrow has perched on its back, or half-expanded wing, in order to gain sufficient elevation to put the food into its mouth. At this advanced stage, I believe that young Cuckoos procure some food for themselves; like the young rook, for instance, which in part feeds itself, and is partly fed by the old ones till the approach of the pairing season. If they did not go off in succession, it is probable we would see them in large numbers by the middle of August; for as they are to be found in great plenty, when in a nestling state, they must now appear very numerous, since all of them must have quitted the nest before this time. But this is not the case; for they are not more numerous at any season than the parent birds are in the months of May and June.

The same instinctive impulse which directs the Cuckoo to deposit her eggs in the nests of other birds, directs her young one to throw out the eggs and young of the owner of the nest. The scheme of nature would be incomplete without it; for it would be extremely difficult, if not impossible, for the little birds, destined to find succour for the Cuckoo, to find it also for their own young ones, after a certain period; nor would there be room for the whole to inhabit the nest.

from 'Observations on the Natural History of the Cuckoo',
Letter to John Hunter FRS, 13 March 1878,
Philosophical Transactions of the Royal Society

The Return of the Birds

JOHN BURROUGHS (1837–1921)

Spring in our northern climate may fairly be said to extend
from the middle of March to the middle of June. At least,
the vernal tide continues to rise until the latter date, and
it is not till after the summer solstice that the shoots and
twigs begin to harden and turn to wood, or the grass to
lose any of its freshness and succulency.

It is this period that marks the return of the birds, –
one or two of the more hardy or half-domesticated species,
like the song sparrow and the bluebird, usually arriving
in March, while the rarer and more brilliant wood-birds
bring up the procession in June. But each stage of the
advancing season gives prominence to certain species, as to
certain flowers. The dandelion tells me when to look for
the swallow, the dogtooth violet when to expect the wood-
thrush, and when I have found the wake-robin in bloom I
know the season is fairly inaugurated. With me this flower
is associated not merely with the awakening of Robin, for
he has been awake for some weeks, but with the universal
awakening and rehabilitation of nature.

Yet the coming and going of the birds is more or less a
mystery and a surprise. We go out in the morning, and no
thrush or vireo is to be heard; we go out again, and every
tree and grove is musical; yet again, and all is silent. Who
saw them come? Who saw them depart?

This pert little winter wren, for instance, darting in and
out the fence, diving under the rubbish here and coming up
yards away, – how does he manage with those little circular
wings to compass degrees and zones, and arrive always in

the nick of time? Last August I saw him in the remotest wilds of the Adirondacks, impatient and inquisitive as usual; a few weeks later, on the Potomac, I was greeted by the same hardy little busybody. Does he travel by easy stages from bush to bush and from wood to wood? or has that compact little body force and courage to brave the night and the upper air, and so achieve leagues at one pull?

And yonder bluebird with the earth tinge on his breast and the sky tinge on his back, – did he come down out of the heaven on that bright March morning when he told us so softly and plaintively that, if we pleased, spring had come? Indeed, there is nothing in the return of the birds more curious and suggestive than in the first appearance, or rumors of the appearance, of this little blue-coat. The bird at first seems a mere wandering voice in the air; one hears its call or carol on some bright March morning, but is uncertain of its source or direction; it falls like a drop of rain when no cloud is visible; one looks and listens, but to no purpose. The weather changes, perhaps a cold snap with snow comes on, and it may be a week before I hear the note again, and this time or the next perchance see this bird sitting on a stake in the fence lifting his wing as he calls cheerily to his mate. Its notes now become daily more frequent; the birds multiply, and, flitting from point to point, call and warble more confidently and gleefully. Their boldness increases till one sees them hovering with a saucy, inquiring air about barns and out-buildings, peeping into dove-cotes and stable windows, inspecting knotholes and pump-trees, intent only on a place to nest. They wage war against robins and wrens, pick quarrels with swallows, and seem to deliberate for days over the policy of taking forcible possession of one of the mud-houses of the latter.

But as the season advances they drift more into the background. Schemes of conquest which they at first seemed bent upon are abandoned, and they settle down very quietly in their old quarters in remote stumpy fields.

Not long after the bluebird comes the robin, sometimes in March, but in most of the Northern States April is the month of the robin. In large numbers they scour the fields and groves. You hear their piping in the meadow, in the pasture, on the hillside. Walk in the woods, and the dry leaves rustle with the whir of their wings, the air is vocal with their cheery call. In excess of joy and vivacity, they run, leap, scream, chase each other through the air, diving and sweeping among the trees with perilous rapidity.

In that free, fascinating, half-work and half-play pursuit, – sugar-making, – a pursuit which still lingers in many parts of New York, as in New England, the robin is one's constant companion. When the day is sunny and the ground bare, you meet him at all points and hear him at all hours. At sunset, on the tops of the tall maples, with look heavenward, and in a spirit of utter abandonment, he carols his simple strain. And sitting thus amid the stark, silent trees, above the wet, cold earth, with the chill of winter still in the air, there is no fitter or sweeter songster in the whole round year. It is in keeping with the scene and the occasion. How round and genuine the notes are, and how eagerly our ears drink them in! The first utterance, and the spell of winter is thoroughly broken, and the remembrance of it afar off.

from *Wake-Robin: The Writings of John Burroughs* (1917)

The Song-Sparrow

CHARLES C. ABBOTT (1843–1919)

All April, when nature saw fit to laugh at our almanacs
and continue winter when and where spring had a better
claim, the song-sparrow took things philosophically and
was just as ready to sing to a dismal blank of leaden sky
as to the brilliant sunrise. A merit of the song not to be
overlooked is that it fits the words of wisdom better than
any nonsense syllables one can coin. There is a sparrow
in my gooseberry-hedge that all day sings, '*Cheer-cheer-
cheer-cheer-cheerfulness.*' … There is nothing of the wren's
excessive nervous energy in the song-sparrow's singing.
The wren, I take it, wants the whole world to hear him;
the song-sparrow's effort is for its own entertainment.

from *In Nature's Realm* (1900)

The Long-Tailed Tit's Nest-Building

EDWARD GREY, *Viscount of Fallodon* (1862–1933)

The most elaborate nest of our common birds, the one on
which the greatest care and labour are expended, is that
of the long-tailed tit. … Long-tailed tits are remarkably
various in their choice of a site. With most birds, we know
to within a few feet the height at which the nest will be
found and the kind of place it will occupy. Long-tailed tits
have two very different types of place. They sometimes
nest in a bush, especially a bush such as whin, juniper or
Rosa rugosa. Here the nest will be only three, four or five
feet above the ground, and with no more solid support

than the twigs of the bush afford. Sometimes the site chosen is the sturdy fork of an oak or ash. In such a place the nest is solidly supported beneath and buttressed by a stout stem on each side. These nests are, in my experience, often high up, and it would need a fairly long ladder to reach them. They are well concealed from eyes below, for they look like a mere thickening of the fork of the tree.

March is the time for finding the nests of the long-tailed tits. The little rattle, which is their most distinctive note, is very frequently uttered and calls attention to the bird. Field-glasses will show whether they have any nesting material in their beaks: if this is so, a very short observation will see the bird go to where the nest is being built.

The morning hours before midday are the business time for nest-building, and with a little care and patience every long-tailed tit's nest in the neighbourhood can be found; according to my observation, the time occupied from the first beginning of the nest to the day when the young leave it is about eleven weeks. This must be nearly or quite double the corresponding period for most little woodland birds. Others more fortunate than myself can say how long it generally takes a pair of these birds to complete a nest; but some notion of the labour and time expended may be formed by considering the number of feathers used in the lining. A friend of mine counted 1,660 separate feathers out of one nest that had been built in his garden; and *British Birds* quotes 1,776 as having been found in one nest. At my sister's house in Hampshire a long-tailed tit, at this stage of its nest-building, was seen to alight on the back of a white turkey cock and pluck a feather from that huge living store.

from *The Charm of Birds* (1927)

Crow Day in New York

WILLIAM BEEBE (1877–1962)

Near New York, a day in March – I have found it varying
from March 8 to March 12 – is 'crow day.' Now the winter
roosts apparently break up, and all day flocks of crows,
sometimes thousands upon thousands of them, pass to
the northward. If the day is quiet and spring-like, they fly
very high, black motes silhouetted against the blue, – but
if the day is a 'March day,' with whistling, howling winds,
then the black fellows fly close to earth, rising just enough
to clear bushes and trees, and taking leeward advantage
of every protection. For days after, many crows pass, but
never so many as on the first day, when crow law, or crow
instinct, passes the word, we know not how, which is
obeyed by all.

For miles around not a drop of water may be found; it
seems as if every pool and lake were solid to the bottom,
and yet, when we see a large bird, with goose-like body,
long neck and long, pointed beak, flying like a bullet of
steel through the sky, we may be sure that there is open
water to the northward, for a loon never makes a mistake.
When the first pioneer of these hardy birds passes, he
knows that somewhere beyond us fish can be caught. If
we wonder where he has spent the long winter months,
we should take a steamer to Florida. Out on the ocean,
sometimes a hundred miles or more from land, many of
these birds make their winter home. When the bow of
the steamer bears down upon one, the bird half spreads
its wings, then closes them quickly, and sinks out of sight
in the green depths, not to reappear until the steamer

has passed, when he looks after us and utters his mocking laugh. Here he will float until the time comes for him to go north. We love the brave fellow, remembering him in his home among the lakes of Canada; but we tremble for him when we think of the terrible storm waves which he must outride, and the sneering sharks which must sometimes spy him. What a story he could tell of his life among the phalaropes and jelly-fishes!

from *The Log of the Sun: A Chronicle of Nature's Year* (1906)

Spring

Edward Thomas (1878–1917)

May 14 Greenfinch laying in a hair-and-moss nest up in the thorns: nest and eggs often like the linnet's, the former usually larger and more careless, the latter larger and with finer markings. While the linnet's eggs are often pearly, the greenfinch's are generally blue.

Bullfinch laying: one pure-white egg among four others, dark-blue with blotches of red and chocolate.

May 21 Chaffinch laying: eggs newly laid on every day of this month: in one case a pale green, without spot or line, unusually frail and dusted with chalk.

June 17 Nightingale hatches her eggs under a bramble: and her mate stops singing and begins to scold with a harsh 'bit-bit' or a wistful 'wheet-torr,' in which both birds join deep in the underwood.

from *The Woodland Life* (1897)

The First Cuckoo

Edward Thomas (1878–1917)

The first snowdrop, the first blackbird's song or peewit's
love cry, the first hawthorn leaves, are as nothing even to
those who regard them, compared with the cuckoo's note,
while there are many for whom it is the one powerfully
significant natural thing throughout the year, apart from
broad gradual changes, such as the greening or the baring
of the woods. The old become fearful lest they should not
hear it: having heard it, they fear lest it should be for the
last time. It has been accepted as the object upon which
we concentrate whatever feeling we have towards the
beginning of spring. It constitutes a natural, unmistakable
festival. We wish to hear it, we are eager and anxious
about it, we pause when it reaches us, as if perhaps it
might be bringing more than it ever brought yet. Vaguely
enough, as a rule, we set much store by this first hearing,
and the expectancy does not fail to bring its reward of at
least a full and intense impression. And for this purpose
the cuckoo's note is perfectly suited. It is loud, clear, brief,
and distinct, never in danger of being lost in a chorus of
its own or another kind: it has a human and also a ghostly
quality which earns it the reputation of sadness or joyous-
ness at different times. ...

When I heard it this April, I could not be wholly
absorbed in it, yet something of me was carried away,
floating in a kind of bliss over the river between the hills.
I had been walking all day in Carmarthenshire in hot,
bright weather. ... Coming over the shoulder of the hill
called Pwll y Pridd, by the farm Morfa Bach, where the

primroses were so thick under the young emerald larches,
I began to have a strong desire – almost amounting to a
conviction – that I should hear the cuckoo. When I was
down again at Goose's Bridge, by the brook that descends
out of a furzy valley towards the Taf, I heard it, or thought
I did. I stopped. Not a sound. I went on stealthily that I
might stop as soon as I heard anything. Again I seemed
to hear it; again it had gone by the time I was still. The
third time I had no doubt. The cuckoo was singing over on
the far side of the valley, perhaps three-quarters of a mile
away, probably in a gorse bank just above the marsh. For
half a minute he sang, changed his perch unseen and sang
again, his notes as free from the dust and heat as the cups
of the marigolds, and as soft as the pale white-blue sky, and
as dim as the valley into whose twilight he was gathered,
calling fainter and fainter, as I drew towards home.

from *The Last Sheaf* (1928)

INLAND
Field, Hedgerow, Pasture, Woodland

All the Birds of Note or Plume in the World

Omar Khayyam (c. 1048–1131)

trans. Edward FitzGerald (1809–1883)

When they had sail'd their Vessel for a Moon,
And marr'd their Beauty with the wind o' th' Sea,
Suddenly in mid Sea reveal'd itself
An Isle, beyond Description beautiful;
An Isle that all was Garden; not a Bird
Of Note or Plume in all the World but there;
There as in Bridal Retinue array'd
The Pheasant in his Crown, the Dove in her Collar;
And those who tuned their Bills among the Trees
That Arm in Arm from Fingers paralyz'd
With any Breath of Air Fruit moist and dry
Down scatter'd in Profusion to their Feet,
Where Fountains of Sweet Water ran, and round
Sunshine and Shadow chequer-chased the Ground.
. . .
Under its Trees in one another's Arms
They slept – they drank its Fountains hand in hand –
Sought Sugar with the Parrot – or in Sport
Paraded with the Peacock – raced the Partridge –
Or fell a-talking with the Nightingale.

from *The Rubáiyát of Omar Khayyám* (1859)

from *The Parlement of Fowles*

GEOFFREY CHAUCER (1340–1400)

And right as Aleyn, in the Pleynt of Kynde,
Devyseth Nature of aray and face,
In swich aray men mighten hir ther finde.
This noble emperesse, ful of grace,
Bad every foul to take his owne place,
As they were wont alwey fro yeer to yere,
Seynt Valentynes day, to stonden there.

That is to sey, the foules of ravyne
Were hyest set; and than the foules smale,
That eten as hem nature wolde enclyne,
As worm or thing of whiche I telle no tale;
And water-foul sat loweste in the dale;
But foul that liveth by seed sat on the grene,
And that so fele, that wonder was to sene.

Ther mighte men the royal egle finde,
That with his sharpe look perceth the sonne;
And other egles of a lower kinde,
Of which that clerkes wel devysen conne.
Ther was the tyraunt with his fethres donne
And greye, I mene the goshauk, that doth pyne
To briddes for his outrageous ravyne.

The gentil faucon, that with his feet distreyneth
The kinges hond; the hardy sperhauk eke,
The quayles foo; the merlion that peyneth
Him-self ful ofte, the larke for to seke;

Ther was the douve, with hir eyen meke;
The jalous swan, ayens his deeth that singeth;
The oule eek, that of deeth the bode bringeth;

The crane the geaunt, with his trompes soune;
The theef, the chogh; and eek the jangling pye;
The scorning jay; the eles foo, the heroune;
The false lapwing, ful of trecherye;
The stare, that the counseyl can biwrey;
The tame ruddok; and the coward kyte;
The cok, that orloge is of thorpes lyte;

The sparow, Venus sone; the nightingale,
That clepeth forth the fresshe leves newe;
The swalow, mordrer of the flyes smale
That maken hony of floures fresshe of hewe
The wedded turtel, with hir herte trewe;
The pecok, with his aungels fethres brighte;
The fesaunt, scorner of the cok by nighte;

The waker goos; the cukkow ever unkinde;
The popinjay, ful of delicasye;
The drake, stroyer of his owne kinde;
The stork, the wreker of avoutrye;
The hote cormeraunt of glotonye;
The raven wys, the crow with vois of care;
The throstel olde; the frosty feldefare.

O Nightingale …

JOHN MILTON (1608–1674)

O Nightingale that on yon bloomy spray
Warblest at eve, when all the woods are still,
Thou with fresh hope the lover's heart dost fill,
While the jolly hours lead on propitious May.
Thy liquid notes that close the eye of day,
First heard before the shallow cuckoo's bill,
Portend success in love. O if Jove's will
Have linked that amorous power to thy soft lay,
Now timely sing, ere the rude bird of hate
Foretell my hopeless doom in some grove nigh;
As thou from year to year hast sung too late
For my relief, yet hadst no reason why.
Whether the Muse, or Love, call thee his mate,
Both them I serve, and of their train am I.

The Larks' Petticoat Government

WILLIAM COBBETT (1763–1835)

On the Sunday morning, before I came away, I walked
about six miles, and … I heard the first singing of the
birds this year; and I here observed an instance of that
petticoat government, which, apparently, pervades the whole
of animated nature. A lark, very near to me in a ploughed
field, rose from the ground, and was saluting the sun with
his delightful song. He was got about as high as the dome
of St. Paul's, having me for a motionless and admiring
auditor, when the hen started up from nearly the same spot
whence the cock had risen, flew up and passed close by
him. I could not hear what she said; but supposed that she
must have given him a pretty smart reprimand; for down
she came upon the ground, and he, ceasing to sing, took
a twirl in the air, and came down after her. Others have,
I dare say, seen this a thousand times over; but I never
observed it before.

from *Rural Rides* (1830)

From the Magpie to the Sparrow

ROBERT BLOOMFIELD (1766–1823)

LITTLE JABBERER,

I have many times thought of addressing to you a few words of advice, as you seem to stand in need of such a friend.

You know that I do not stand much upon ceremony; I am always ready for talking and for giving advice, and really wonder how other birds can keep themselves so quiet. Then you will pardon my frankness, since you know my character, when I inform you, that I think you remarkably tame and spiritless: you have no enterprise in you. In an old farm-yard, shuffling amongst the straw, there you may be found morning, noon, and night; and you are never seen in the woods, and groves, with me and my companions, where we have the blessing of free liberty, and fly where we please. You must often have heard me sing; that cannot be doubted, because I am heard a great way. As to me, I never come down to your farm, unless I think I can find a hen's egg or two amongst the nettles, or a chicken or duck just hatched.

I earnestly advise you to change your manner of life, and take a little free air, as I do. Stop no longer in your dull yard, feeding upon pigs' leavings, but come abroad with me. – But I must have done, till a better opportunity; for the gamekeeper with his gun has just turned the corner. Take my advice, and you may be as well off, and learn to sing as well as I do.

Yours, in great haste,

Mag.

from *The Remains of Robert Bloomfield* (1824)

A Raven in Bainriggs Wood

DOROTHY WORDSWORTH (1771–1855)

Sunday, 27th [*June*].— … After tea we rowed down to
Loughrigg Fell, visited the white foxglove, gathered wild
strawberries, and walked up to view Rydale. We lay a
long time looking at the lake; the shores all dim with the
scorching sun. The ferns were turning yellow, that is,
here and there one was quite turned. We walked round
by Benson's wood home. The lake was now most still,
and reflected the beautiful yellow and blue and purple and
grey colours of the sky. We heard a strange sound in the
Bainriggs wood, as we were floating on the water; it *seemed*
in the wood, but it must have been above it, for presently
we saw a raven very high above us. It called out, and the
dome of the sky seemed to echo the sound. It called again
and again as it flew onwards, and the mountains gave
back the sound, seeming as if from their centre; a musical
bell-like answering to the bird's hoarse voice. We heard
both the call of the bird, and the echo, after we could see
him no longer.…

from *Journals of Dorothy Wordsworth*

All the Birds in Grove or Glen
James Jennings of Huntspill (1772–1833)

Oh, how shall description with pencil or pen
Pourtray all the Birds now in grove or in glen!
Here the trees' bending branches the Perchers possess;
There the Waders and Swimmers the waters caress;
While the Scratchers of Earth sought a worm;
 with a bound
The Snatchers flew swiftly aloft and around.
  The Lord of the boundless bright realm of the Air,
With his broad sweeping wing, the proud Eagle,
 was there.
His cere and his feet ting'd with yellowish gold;
At once he appear'd both majectic and bold:
With an eye, beak, and talons, that fierceness express,
Yet both plumage and air what is noble confess, –
 A mien most imposing – a monarch supreme.
The Swan, too, sailed stately adown the clear stream;
His plumes of fair white and arch'd neck to display,
While the Cygnets beside him appear'd in ash-grey.
There were Fieldfares in troops; of the Missel-Thrush
 few;
These their songs on the elm now and then would renew.
 The warbling *cock* Blackbird, with deep yellow bill,
Was pleas'd his loud notes in rich cadence to trill;
Where the waters forth gushing, in murmurs down fell,
The Thrush a sweet music pour'd out in the dell.
While all breathless and silent crept softly delight
To listen with day to the Songster of Night:

In a thick, hazel copse he was warbling apart
Such notes as have never been equall'd by art.
That bird for whom many a harp hath been strung; –
Whose warble enraptures the old and the young; –
With feeling's soft touch wakes the poet's sweet lyre,
And the pensive, the tender, doth often inspire.

from Ornithologia, or The Birds (1828)

Of Pigeons
COUNTRY GENTLEMAN (*18th century*)

Pigeons have several natures and names. The tame or
house pigeons are called barbels, jacks, crappers, carriers,
runts, horsemen, tumblers, and great reds; the barbel
has a red eye, a short tail, and a bill like a bullfinch; the
small jack pigeon is a good breeder, and hardy, and has a
turned crown; the crappers are valuable for their swell;
the carriers for their swift return home, if carried to a
distance; the horseman is something of the carrier's nature;
the tumblers for their pleasant agility in the air; the runts
for their good breeding, and bringing up their young ones;
the great red for their largeness; the turntails for their
turning them up almost to their backs; and the black head
is a white pigeon with a black head. Several of these are
often preferred for their beauty, but the most common
are the runts. Generally, in about half a year's time, the
young ones may be paired, by putting a cock and a hen
into a small coop hutch, where sometimes in an hour or
two, and sometimes not under a day, two, or three, they
will pair, which is known by their billing and cooing, the

cock calling the hen, and the hen spreading herself before him. They breed almost all the year except moulting time. It is common to cross match them, and they will breed the better; and should be fed all the year, except feed time and harvest: the former holds about a month, and the latter three, even to Alhollandtide. … They commonly hatch within three weeks, lay generally two eggs, and about three weeks after hatching they are fit for market.

from *The Complete Grazier: or, Gentleman and Farmer's Directory* (1776)

In Any Sequestered Woodland

CHARLES KINGSLEY (1819–1875)

But listen to the charm of birds in any sequestered woodland, on a bright forenoon in June. As you try to disentangle the medley of sounds, the first, perhaps, which will strike your ear will be the loud, harsh, monotonous, flippant song of the chaffinch; and the metallic clinking of two or three sorts of titmice. But above the tree-tops, rising, hovering, sinking, the woodlark is fluting, tender and low. Above the pastures outside the skylark sings – as he alone can sing; and close by, from the hollies rings out the blackbird's tenor – rollicking, audacious, humorous, all but articulate. From the tree above him rises the treble of the thrush, pure as the song of angels: more pure, perhaps, in tone, though neither so varied nor so rich, as the song of the nightingale. And there, in the next holly, is the nightingale himself: now croaking like a frog; now talking aside to his wife on the nest below; and now bursting out into that song, or cycle of songs, in which if any man finds

sorrow, he himself surely finds none. All the morning
he will sing; and again at evening, till the small hours,
and the chill before the dawn: but if his voice sounds
melancholy at night, heard all alone, or only mocked by the
ambitious black-cap, it sounds in the bright morning that
which it is, the fulness of joy and love. Milton's

'Sweet bird, that shun'st the noise of folly,
    Most musical, most melancholy,'

is untrue to fact. So far from shunning the noise of folly,
the nightingale sings as boldly as anywhere close to a
stage-coach road, or a public path, as anyone will testify
who recollects the 'Wrangler's Walk' from Cambridge to
Trumpington forty years ago, when the covert, which has
now become hollow and shelterless, held, at every twenty
yards, an unabashed and jubilant nightingale.

from *Prose Idylls, New and Old* (1882)

The Cockatoo and the Kanary-Nut

Alfred Russel Wallace (1823–1913)

I will here relate something of the habits of this bird, with
which I have since become acquainted. It frequents the
lower parts of the forest, and is seen singly, or at most two
or three together. It flies slowly and noiselessly, and may
be killed by a comparatively slight wound. It eats various
fruits and seeds, but seems more particularly attached
to the kernel of the kanary-nut, which grows on a lofty
forest tree (*Canarium commune*), abundant in the islands
where this bird is found; and the manner in which it gets

at these seeds shows a correlation of structure and habits, which would point out the 'kanary' as its special food. The shell of this nut is so excessively hard that only a heavy hammer will crack it; it is somewhat triangular, and the outside is quite smooth. The manner in which the bird opens these nuts is very curious. Taking one endways in its bill and keeping it firm by a pressure of the tongue, it cuts a transverse notch by a lateral sawing motion of the sharp-edged lower mandible. This done, it takes hold of the nut with its foot, and biting off a piece of leaf retains it in the deep notch of the upper mandible, and again seizing the nut, which is prevented from slipping by the elastic tissue of the leaf, fixes the edge of the lower mandible in the notch, and by a powerful nip breaks off a piece of the shell, again taking the nut in its claws, it inserts the very long and sharp point of the bill and picks out the kernel, which is seized hold of, morsel by morsel, by the extensible tongue. Thus every detail of form and structure in the extraordinary bill of this bird seems to have its use, and we may easily conceive that the black cockatoos have maintained themselves in competition with their more active and more numerous white allies, by their power of existing on a kind of food which no other bird is able to extract from its stony shell. The species is the *Microglossum aterrimum* of naturalists.

from *The Malay Archipelago: The Land of the Orang-Utan, and the Bird of Paradise* (1869)

A bird came down the walk

EMILY DICKINSON (1830–1886)

A bird came down the walk:
He did not know I saw;
He bit an angle-worm in halves
And ate the fellow, raw.

And then he drank a dew
From a convenient grass,
And then hopped sidewise to the wall
To let a beetle pass.

He glanced with rapid eyes
That hurried all abroad, –
They looked like frightened beads, I thought;
He stirred his velvet head

Like one in danger; cautious,
I offered him a crumb,
And he unrolled his feathers
And rowed him softer home

Than oars divide the ocean,
Too silver for a seam,
Or butterflies, off banks of noon,
Leap, plashless, as they swim.

The Woodpecker's Nest

John Burroughs (1837–1921)

I shall never forget the circumstances of observing a pair of
yellow-bellied woodpeckers – the most rare and secluded,
and, next to the red-headed, the most beautiful species
found in our woods – breeding in an old, truncated beech in
the Beaverkill Mountains, an offshoot of the Catskills. We
had been traveling, three of us, all day in search of a trout
lake, which lay far in among the mountains, had twice lost
our course in the trackless forest, and, weary and hungry,
had sat down to rest upon a decayed log. The chattering of
the young, and the passing to and fro of the parent birds,
soon arrested my attention. The entrance to the nest was
on the east side of the tree, about twenty-five feet from the
ground. At intervals of scarcely a minute, the old birds, one
after the other, would alight upon the edge of the hole with
a grub or worm in their beaks; then each in turn would
make a bow or two, cast an eye quickly around, and by
a single movement place itself in the neck of the passage.
Here it would pause a moment, as if to determine in which
expectant mouth to place the morsel, and then disappear
within. In about half a minute, during which time that
chattering of the young gradually subsided, the bird would
again emerge, but this time bearing in its beak the ordure of
one of the helpless family. Flying away very slowly with head
lowered and extended, as if anxious to hold the offensive
object as far from its plumage as possible, the bird dropped
the unsavory morsel in the course of a few yards, and,
alighting on a tree, wiped its bill on the bark and moss.

from *Wake-Robin* (1917)

The Line of the Hedge

RICHARD JEFFERIES (1848–1887)

There seemed just now the tiniest twinkle of movement
by the rushes, but it was lost among the hedge parsley.
Among the grey leaves of the willow there is another flit
of motion; and visible now against the sky there is a little
brown bird, not to be distinguished at the moment from
the many other little brown birds that are known to be
about. He got up into the willow from the hedge parsley
somehow, without being seen to climb or fly. Suddenly he
crosses to the tops of the hawthorn and immediately flings
himself up into the air a yard or two, his wings and ruffled
crest making a ragged outline; jerk, jerk, jerk, as if it
were with the utmost difficulty he could keep even at that
height. He scolds, and twitters, and chirps, and all at once
sinks like a stone into the hedge and out of sight as a stone
into a pond. It is a whitethroat; his nest is deep in the
parsley and nettles. Presently he will go out to the island
apple tree and back again in a minute or two; the pair of
them are so fond of each other's affectionate company, they
cannot remain apart.

Watching the line of the hedge, about every two
minutes, either near at hand or yonder a bird darts out just
at the level of the grass, hovers a second with labouring
wings, and returns as swiftly to the cover. Sometimes it
is a flycatcher, sometimes a greenfinch, or chaffinch, now
and then a robin, in one place a shrike, perhaps another is
a redstart. They are flyfishing all of them, seizing insects
from the sorrel tips and grass, as the kingfisher takes a
roach from the water. A blackbird slips up into the oak and

a dove descends in the corner by the chestnut tree. But these are not visible together, only one at a time and with intervals. The larger part of the life of the hedge is out of sight. All the thrush-fledglings, the young blackbirds, and finches are hidden, most of them on the mound among the ivy, and parsley, and rough grasses, protected, too, by a roof of brambles. The nests that still have eggs are not, like the nests of the early days of April, easily found; they are deep down in the tangled herbage by the shore of the ditch, or far inside the thorny thickets which then looked mere bushes, and are now so broad. Landrails are running in the grass concealed as a man would be in a wood; they have nests and eggs on the ground for which you may search in vain till the mowers come.

from *The Pageant of Summer* (1901)

Skylarks over the Trenches
Saki (H.H. Munro) (1870–1916)

Considering the enormous economic dislocation which the war operations have caused in the regions where the campaign is raging, there seems to be very little corresponding disturbance in the bird life of the same districts. Rats and mice have mobilized and swarmed into the fighting line, and there has been a partial mobilization of owls, particularly barn owls, following in the wake of the mice, and making laudable efforts to thin out their numbers. What success attends their hunting one cannot estimate; there are always sufficient mice left over to populate one's dug-out and make a parade-ground and race-course of one's face at night. In the matter of nesting accommodation the barn owls are well provided for; most of the still intact barns in the war zone are requisitioned for billeting purposes, but there is a wealth of ruined houses … here in Northern France the owls have desolation and mice at their disposal in unlimited quantities, and as these birds breed in winter as well as in summer, there should be a goodly output of war owlets to cope with the swarming generations of war mice. Apart from the owls one cannot notice that the campaign is making any marked difference in the bird life of the country-side. …

The skylark in this region has stuck tenaciously to the meadows and croplands that have been seamed and bisected with trenches and honeycombed with shell-holes. In the chill, misty hour of gloom that precedes a rainy dawn, when nothing seemed alive except a few wary waterlogged sentries and many scuttling rats, the lark would suddenly dash skyward and pour forth a song of ecstatic jubilation that sounded horribly forced and insincere. It seemed scarcely possible that the bird could carry its insouciance to the length of attempting to rear a brood in that desolate wreckage of shattered clods and gaping shell-holes, but once, having occasion to throw myself down with some abruptness on my face, I found myself nearly on the top of a brood of young larks. Two of them had already been hit by something, and were in rather a battered condition, but the survivors seemed as tranquil and comfortable as the average nestling.

At the corner of a stricken wood (which has had a name made for it in history, but shall be nameless here), at a moment when lyddite and shrapnel and machine-gun

fire swept and raked and bespattered that devoted spot as
though the artillery of an entire Division had suddenly con-
centrated on it, a wee hen-chaffinch flitted wistfully to and
fro, amid splintered and falling branches that had never a
green bough left on them. The wounded lying there, if any
of them noticed the small bird, may well have wondered
why anything having wings and no pressing reason for
remaining should have chosen to stay in such a place. There
was a battered orchard alongside the stricken wood, and
the probable explanation of the bird's presence was that it
had a nest of young ones whom it was too scared to feed,
too loyal to desert. Later on, a small flock of chaffinches
blundered into the wood, which they were doubtless in the
habit of using as a highway to their feeding-grounds; unlike
the solitary hen-bird, they made no secret of their desire
to get away as fast as their dazed wits would let them. The
only other bird I ever saw there was a magpie, flying low
over the wreckage of fallen tree-limbs; 'one for sorrow',
says the old superstition. There was sorrow enough in that
wood.

from 'Birds on the Western Front' (1916)

The Wood-Pigeons Come Home

EDWARD THOMAS (1878–1917)

They were the gentlest of chalk hills crested with trees –
Thrift Hill, Gallows Hill, Crouch Hill, Pott's Hill, Rain
Hill, Wheat Hill, Windmill Hill, and Weston Hills – and
at their highest points there were villages, like Therfield,
Kelshall, Sandon, Wallington, Clothall, Weston. I had still
four or five miles to walk at the feet of these hills, through
a silence undisturbed by the few market carts at long
intervals. ... A wood-pigeon came sloping down from the
far sky with fewer and fewer wing strokes and longer and
longer glidings upon half-closed wings as it drew near its
home tree. It disappeared; another flew in sight and slanted
downward with the same 'folding-in' motion; and then
another. The air was silent and still, the road was empty.
The birds coming home to the quiet earth seemed visitors
from another world. They seemed to bring something out
of the sky down to this world, and the house and garden
where I stayed at last were full of this something.

from *The Icknield Way* (1916)

Dancing Cranes

H.C.I. (*20th century*)

28 May 1904

Among 'animals which play games' the *saras*, or Indian crane (*Ardea Antigone*), is, I think, entitled to a place. Some twelve or fourteen years ago, in the Shahjahanpur district of Rohilkhand, I witnessed a dance by three of these birds, in which one, a female, stood in the centre while the other two, males, described figures of eight round her, all three bowing to one another at regular intervals. ... I have also seen what I can only describe as a boxing match between two of these cranes, which was a most ludicrous sight. Twelve or fifteen *saras* formed a ring, in the middle of which the two combatants fought a number of rounds, squaring up at each other with their wings, and striking blows which could be heard several hundred yards off. There was no biting or kicking, nothing but honest boxing with the wings. Each round lasted perhaps a minute or more, and in the intervals the two combatants strolled about in the ring until time was up, when they went at it again. I sat on my horse watching the fight for at least ten minutes, at the end of which the ring broke up and the birds dispersed.

Letter to *The Spectator*

A White-Collared Blackbird

GILLIAN CLARKE (1937–)

Yet all the shortening day, from here at the table as I write,
there is enough light to watch the birds: a greater spotted
woodpecker brightening the show among the common
crowd at the feeder; a heron, sudden and low over Allt
Maen's field; a kite over the garden so close we look each
other in the eye. Just now a huge flock of starlings passing
over the garden, low and close, a whirring shoal that
divides and merges into one again.

And the blackbird. In winter there is always a female
blackbird on the forage. This year she is the distinctive bird
with her necklace of white beads, white cheek freckles and
a scrap of white lace on her head. She appeared last winter,
nested in the hedge by the lane, raised a brood of fledg-
lings, withdrew in July, and is now here every day. When I
first saw her I feared that her strange marking might single
her out as a freak and that she might be rejected by the
other birds. But she is sociable, and her mate is an ordinary
blackbird, black and handsome, foraging beside her in the
bark mulch. I've heard it said that every blackbird has one
white feather somewhere in its plumage, like a flake of
snow.

from *At the Source* (2008)

BIRD SONG
& *Songsters*

Of Birds that Speak

PLINY THE ELDER (C. 23–79 CE)

The Carduelis is the smallest of Birds; and they execute
Commands, not only with their Voice, but also with their
Feet and Mouth, as if they were Hands. In the Territory
of Arelate, there is a Bird called Taurus, because it loweth
like a Bull, although otherwise a small Bird. There is
another also named Anthus, which imitates the neighing
of Horses; and if by the Approach of Horses it is driven
from their Grass on which it feeds, it will neigh, and so be
revenged of them. But above all other Things they repeat
human Language, and the Psittaci even hold a Conversation. This Bird cometh from India, where they call it
Sittace. It is green all over the Body, only it hath a distinct
Collar about the Neck of vermilion red. The Parrot salutes
Emperors, and pronounces what Words she heareth; she is
also very wanton under the Influence of Wine. Her Head is
as hard as her Beak. When she learns to speak, she must be
beaten about the Head with a Rod of Iron: for otherwise
she careth for no Blows. When she taketh her Flight
downward, she alighteth upon her Bill, and leans upon it,
and by that means favoureth her Feet, which are but feeble.

There is a kind of Pica (Magpie) of less excellency,
because she does not come from so far; but she pro-
nounceth what is taught her more freely and distinctly.
These take a Love to the Words they speak; for they not
only learn them, but they delight in them: insomuch that
they study them inwardly, and by their careful thinking
upon what they learn, they show how attentive they are. It
is known that they have died for Grief that they could not

conquer the Difficulty of some Words; as also, that unless they hear the same Words repeated often, their Memory fails to retain them. If they are in search of a Word, and chance to hear it pronounced, they will show wonderful Signs of Joy. Their Beauty is not ordinary, although not very lovely. But they are handsome enough in the Power to imitate human Speech.

It is said, that none of their kind are able to learn, except such only as feed upon Mast; and among them, those acquire the more easily that have five toes to their Feet: but not even these unless in the two first Years of their Age. Their Tongue is broader than ordinary: as they are all in every separate kind that counterfeit Man's Voice: although this happens to almost all Birds. Agrippina, the Wife of Claudius Caesar, had a Turdus (Thrush) at the Time I compiled this Book, which imitated Man's Speech; a Thing never known before. The young Caesars, also, had a Sturnus (Starling) and Nightingales taught to speak Greek and Latin. Moreover, they would study their Lessons all Day, and continually come out with new Words formed into a long Speech. To teach them, these Birds must be in a Place apart, where they can hear no other Voice to mingle with what they learn; and one is to sit by them, who must repeat often what he would have them fix in their Memory, and please them also with giving them Meat.

from *Natural History* (77 CE), based on a
1601 translation by Philemon Holland

The Goldfinch and the Nightingale

ANON (*formerly attributed to* GEOFFREY CHAUCER)

And as I stood, and cast aside mine eye,
I was ware of the fairest medlar tree
That ever yet in all my life I seye,
As full of blossoms as it mighte be;
Therein a goldfinch leaping prettily
From bough to bough; and as him list he eat
Here and there of the buds and flowers sweet.

And to the arbour side was adjoining
This fairest tree, of which I have you told;
And at the last the bird began to sing
(When he had eaten what he eate wo'ld)
So passing sweetly, that by many fold
It was more pleasant than I could devise;
And, when his song was ended in this wise,

The nightingale with so merry a note
Answered him, that all the woode rung,
So suddenly, that, as it were a sote
I stood astound'; so was I with the song
Thorough ravished, that, till late and long,
I wist not in what place I was, nor where;
Again, me thought, she sung e'en by mine ear.

from *The Floure and the Leaf* (*c.* 1460–80)

When the Ravens Could Speak

ANON

Once, long ago, there was a time when the ravens could talk.

But the strange thing about the ravens' speech was that their words had the opposite meaning. When they wanted to thank any one, they used words of abuse, and thus always said the reverse of what they meant.

But as they were thus so full of lies, there came one day an old man, and by magic means took away their power of speech. And since that time the ravens can do no more than shriek.

But the ravens' nature has not changed, and to this day they are an ill-tempered, lying, thieving lot.

from Eskimo Folk-Tales, collected by Knud Rasmussen (1921)

The Language of Birds

GILBERT WHITE (1720–1793)

Selborne, Sept. 9, 1778.
The language of birds is very ancient, and, like other ancient modes of speech, very elliptical: little is said, but much is meant and understood.

The notes of the eagle-kind are shrill and piercing; and about the season of nidification much diversified, as I have been often assured by a curious observer of nature, who long resided at Gibraltar, where eagles abound. The notes of our hawks much resemble those of the king of birds. Owls have very expressive notes; they hoot in a fine vocal sound, much resembling the *vox humana*, and reducible by a pitch-pipe to a musical key. This note seems to express complacency and rivalry among the males: they use also a quick call and an horrible scream; and can snore and hiss when they mean to menace. Ravens, beside their loud croak, can exert a deep and solemn note that makes the woods to echo; the amorous sound of a crow is strange and ridiculous; rooks, in the breeding season, attempt sometimes in the gaiety of their hearts to sing, but with no great success; the parrot-kind have many modulations of voice, as appears by their aptitude to learn human sounds; doves coo in an amorous and mournful manner, and are emblems of despairing lovers; the wood-pecker sets up a sort of loud and hearty laugh; the fern-owl, or goat-sucker, from the dusk till day-break, serenades his mate with the clattering of castanets. All the tuneful *passeres* express their complacency by sweet modulations, and a variety of melody. The swallow, as has been observed in a former letter, by a shrill alarm bespeaks the attention of the other hirundines, and bids them be aware that the hawk is at hand. Aquatic and gregarious birds, especially the nocturnal, that shift their quarters in the dark, are very noisy and loquacious; as cranes, wild-geese, wild-ducks, and the like; their perpetual clamour prevents them from dispersing and losing their companions.

In so extensive a subject, sketches and outlines are as much as can be expected; for it would be endless to instance in all the infinite variety of the feathered nation. We shall therefore confine the remainder of this letter to the few domestic fowls of our yards, which are most known, and therefore best understood. At first the peacock, with his gorgeous train, demands our attention; but, like most of the gaudy birds, his notes are grating and shocking to the ear: the yelling of cats, and the braying of an ass, are not more disgustful. The voice of the goose is trumpet-like, and clanking; and once saved the Capitol at Rome, as grave historians assert: the hiss also of the gander is formidable and full of menace, and 'protective of his young'. Among ducks the sexual distinction of voice is remarkable; for, while the quack of the female is loud and sonorous, the voice of the drake is inward and harsh and feeble, and scarce discernible. The cock turkey struts and gobbles to his mistress in a most uncouth manner; he hath also a pert and petulant note when he attacks his adversary. When a hen turkey leads forth her young brood she keeps a watchful eye: and if a bird of prey appear, though ever so high in the air, the careful mother announces the enemy with a little inward moan, and watches him with a steady and attentive look; but if he approach, her note becomes earnest and alarming, and her outcries are redoubled.

No inhabitants of a yard seem possessed of such a variety of expression and so copious a language as common poultry. Take a chicken of four or five days old, and hold it up to a window where there are flies, and it will immediately seize its prey, with little twitterings of complacency; but if you tender it a wasp or a bee, at once its note becomes harsh, and expressive of disapprobation and a sense of danger. When a pullet is ready to lay she intimates the event by a joyous and easy soft note. Of all the occurrences of their life that of laying seems to be the most important; for no sooner has a hen disburdened herself, than she rushes forth with a clamorous kind of joy, which

the cock and the rest of his mistresses immediately adopt.
The tumult is not confined to the family concerned, but
catches from yard to yard, and spreads to every homestead
within hearing, till at last the whole village is in an uproar.
As soon as a hen becomes a mother her new relation
demands a new language; she then runs clucking and
screaming about, and seems agitated as if possessed. The
father of the flock has also a considerable vocabulary; if he
finds food, he calls a favourite concubine to partake; and if
a bird of prey passes over, with a warning voice he bids his
family beware. The gallant chanticleer has, at command,
his amorous phrases, and his terms of defiance. But the
sound by which he is best known is his crowing: by this he
has been distinguished in all ages as the countryman's clock
or larum, as the watchman that proclaims the divisions of
the night.

from Letter to the Honourable Daines Barrington,
The Natural History of Selborne (1789)

Summer's Song-Birds

GILBERT WHITE (1720–1793)

Selborne, Sept. 2, 1774.
The note of the white-throat, which is continually
repeated, and often attended with odd gesticulations on
the wing, is harsh and displeasing. These birds seem of a
pugnacious disposition; for they sing with an erected crest
and attitudes of rivalry and defiance; are shy and wild in
breeding-time, avoiding neighbourhoods, and haunting
lonely lanes and commons; nay even the very tops of the

Sussex-downs, where there are bushes and covert; but in July and August they bring their broods into gardens and orchards, and make great havoc among the summer-fruits.

The black-cap has in common a full, sweet, deep, loud and wild pipe; yet that strain is of short continuance, and his motions are desultory; but when that bird sits calmly and engages in song in earnest, he pours forth very sweet, but inward melody, and expresses great variety of soft and gentle modulations, superior perhaps to those of any of our warblers, the nightingale excepted.

Black-caps mostly haunt orchards and gardens; while they warble their throats are wonderfully distended.

The song of the red-start is superior, though somewhat like that of the white-throat: some birds have a few more notes than others. Sitting very placidly on the top of a tree in a village, the cock sings from morning to night: he affects neighbourhoods, and avoids solitude, and loves to build in orchards and about houses; with us he perches on the vane of a tall maypole.

The fly-catcher is of all our summer birds the most mute and the most familiar: it also appears the last of any. It builds in a vine, or a sweetbriar, against the wall of an house, or in the hole of a wall, or on the end of a beam or plate, and often close to the post of a door where people are going in and out all day long. This bird does not make the least pretension to song, but uses a little inward wailing note when it thinks its young in danger from cats or other annoyances: it breeds but once, and retires early.

from Letter to Thomas Pennant, Esquire,
The Natural History of Selborne (1789)

To the Owl

ROBERT BURNS (1759–1796)

Sad bird of Night, what sorrows call thee forth,
    To vent thy plaints thus in the midnight hour;
Is it some blast that gathers in the north,
    Threat'ning to nip the verdure of thy bow'r?

Is it, sad Owl, that Autumn strips the shade,
    And leaves thee here, unshelter'd and forlorn?
Or fear that Winter will thy nest invade?
    Or friendless Melancholy bids thee mourn?

Shut out, lone Bird, from all the feathered train,
    To tell thy sorrows to th' unheeding gloom;
No friend to pity when thou dost complain,
    Grief all thy thought, and solitude thy home.

Sing on, sad mourner! I will bless thy strain,
    And pleased in sorrow listen to thy song:
Sing on, sad mourner! to the night complain,
    While the lone echo wafts thy notes along.

Is beauty less, when down the glowing cheek
    Sad, piteous tears, in native sorrows fall?
Less kind the heart when anguish bids it break?
    Less happy he who lists to Pity's call?

Ah no, sad owl! nor is thy voice less sweet,
    That sadness tunes it, and that Grief is there;
That Spring's gay notes unskill'd, thou canst repeat;
    That Sorrow bids thee to the gloom repair.

Nor that the treble songsters of the day
    Are quite estranged, sad Bird of night! from thee;
Nor that the thrush deserts the evening spray,
    When darkness calls thee from thy reverie.

From some old tower, thy melancholy dome,
    While the grey walls and desert solitudes
Return each note, responsive to the gloom
    Of ivied coverts and surrounding woods;

There hooting, I will list more pleased to thee
    Than ever lover to the nightingale;
Or drooping wretch, oppress'd with misery,
    Lending his ear to some condoling tale.

The Ibis's Alarm Call

David Livingstone (1813–1873)

In passing along under the overhanging trees of the banks, we often saw the pretty turtle-doves sitting peacefully on their nests above the roaring torrent. An ibis had perched her home on the end of a stump. Her loud, harsh scream of 'Wa-wa-wa', and the piping of the fish-hawk, are sounds which can never be forgotten by any one who has sailed on the rivers north of 20 Deg. south. If we step on shore, the 'Charadrius caruncula', a species of plover, a most plaguy sort of 'public-spirited individual', follows you, flying overhead, and is most persevering in its attempts to give fair warning to all the animals within hearing to flee from the approaching danger. The alarm-note, 'tinc-tinc-tinc', of another variety of the same family (*Pluvianus armatus* of Burchell) has so much of a metallic ring, that this bird is called 'setula-tsipi', or hammering-iron. It is furnished with a sharp spur on its shoulder, much like that on the heel of a cock, but scarcely half an inch in length. Conscious of power, it may be seen chasing the white-necked raven with great fury, and making even that comparatively large bird call out from fear.

from *Missionary Travels and Researches in South Africa* (1857)

The Midnight Songster

JOHN RUSKIN (1819–1900)

An extraordinary scene is to be witnessed every evening
at Leicester in the freemen's allotment gardens, where a
nightingale has established itself. The midnight songster
was first heard a week ago, and every evening hundreds
of people line the roads near the trees where the bird has
his haunt. The crowds patiently wait till the music begins,
and the bulk of the listeners remain till midnight, while
a number of enthusiasts linger till one and two o'clock in
the morning. Strange to say, the bird usually sings in a
large thorn bush just over the mouth of the tunnel of the
Midland main line, but the songster is heedless of noise,
and smoke, and steam, his stream of song being uninter-
rupted for four or five hours every night. So large has been
the throng of listeners that the chief constable has drafted
a number of policemen to maintain order and prevent
damage.   – *Pall Mall Gazette*, May 11th, 1889.

from *Præterita III* (1899)

The Singing of Mocking-Birds

CHARLES ELIOT NORTON (1827–1908)

To J.R. Lowell
MIDWAY, EDISTO ISLAND.
Good Friday Night, April 6, 1855.

… We are some thirty miles south of Charleston, and to
the softness of the Southern climate is added the luxury
of sea air. … Think of being woke up in the morning as
I was yesterday and shall be to-morrow by the singing of
mocking-birds on a tree that grows near my window. Such
a flood of song as they pour out would drown the music
of all the nightingales that ever sang on the Brenta. Their
song is the true essence of all sweet summer sounds, so
rich in melody, so various, so soft and delicate and then so
loud and joyful that nothing more exquisite was ever heard
even in the enchanted gardens of romance.

High from the earth I heard a bird

EMILY DICKINSON (1830—1886)

High from the earth I heard a bird;
   He trod upon the trees
As he esteemed them trifles,
   And then he spied a breeze,
And situated softly
   Upon a pile of wind
Which in a perturbation
   Nature had left behind.
A joyous-going fellow
   I gathered from his talk,
Which both of benediction
   And badinage partook,
Without apparent burden,
   I learned, in leafy wood
He was the faithful father
   Of a dependent brood;
And this untoward transport
   His remedy for care, —
A contrast to our respites.
   How different we are!

A Rollicking Polyglot

JOHN BURROUGHS (1837–1921)

I seldom go the Rock Creek route without being amused
and sometimes annoyed by the yellow-breasted chat. This
bird also has something of the manners and build of the
catbird, yet he is truly an original. The catbird is mild
and feminine compared with this rollicking polyglot. His
voice is very loud and strong and quite uncanny. No sooner
have you penetrated his retreat, which is usually a thick
undergrowth in low, wet localities, near the woods or
in old fields, than he begins his serenade, which for the
variety, grotesqueness, and uncouthness of the notes is not
unlike a country *skimmerton*. If one passes directly along,
the bird may scarcely break the silence. But pause a while,
or loiter quietly about, and your presence stimulates him to
do his best. He peeps quizzically at you from beneath the
branches, and gives a sharp feline mew. In a moment more
he says very distinctly, *who*, *who*. Then in rapid succession
follow notes the most discordant that ever broke the sylvan
silence. Now he barks like a puppy, then quacks like a
duck, then rattles like a kingfisher, then squalls like a fox,
then caws like a crow, then mews like a cat. Now he calls
as if to be heard a long way off, then changes his key, as if
addressing the spectator. Though very shy, and carefully
keeping himself screened when you show any disposition
to get a better view, he will presently, if you remain quiet,
ascend a twig, or hop out on a branch in plain sight, lop
his tail, droop his wings, cock his head, and become very
melodramatic. In less than half a minute he darts into the
bushes again, and again tunes up, no Frenchman rolling his

r's so fluently. *C-r-r-r-r-r — Wrrr, — that's it, — chee, — quack, cluck, — yit-yit-yit, — now hit it, — tr-r-r-r, — when, — caw, caw, — cut, cut, — tea-boy, — who, who, — mew, mew, —* and so on till you are tired of listening.

from *Wake-Robin* (1917)

The Heronry

W.H. HUDSON (1841–1922)

The heron is a bird with a big voice. When nest-building is going on, and in fact until most of the eggs are laid, herons are noisy birds, and the sounds they emit are most curious – the loud familiar squalk or 'frank', which resembles the hard, powerful alarm-note of the peacock, but is more harsh, while other grinding metallic cries remind one of the carrion-crow. Other of their loud sounds are distinctly mammalian in character; there is a dog-like sound, partly bark and partly yelp, swine-like grunting, and other sounds which recall the peculiar, unhappy, desolate cries of the large felines, especially of the puma. One need not take it for granted that these strange vocal noises are nothing but love calls. They may be in part expressions of anger, since it is hardly to be believed that the members of these rude communities invariably respect one another's rights. We see how it is with the rook, which has a more developed social instinct than the lonely savage heron.

During incubation quiet reigns in the heronry; when the young are out, especially when they are well grown and ravenously hungry all day long, the wood is again filled with the uproar; and a noisier heronry than the one I am describing could not have been found. For one thing, it was situated on the very edge of the wood, overlooking the green flat expanse towards Breydon Water, where the parent birds did most of their fishing, so that the returning birds were visible from the tree-tops at a great distance, travelling slowly with eel- and frog- and fish-laden gullets on their wide-spread blue wings – dark blue against the high shining blue of the sky. All the young birds, stretched up to their full height, would watch its approach, and each and every one of them would regard the returning bird as its own too-long absent parent with food to appease its own furious hunger; and as it came sweeping over the colony there would be a tremendous storm of wild expectant cries – strange cat- and dog-like growling, barking, yelping, whining, screaming; and this would last until the newcomer would drop upon its own tree and nest and feed its own young, whereupon the tempest would slowly subside, only to be renewed on the appearance of the next great blue bird coming down over the wood.

from *The Book of a Naturalist* (1919)

A Shy Woodland Thrush in Rio

THEODORE ROOSEVELT (1858–1919)

In the dense tropical woods near Rio Janeiro I heard, in late October – springtime near the southern tropic – the songs of many birds that I could not identify. But the most beautiful music was from a shy woodland thrush, sombre-coloured, which lived near the ground in the thick timber, but sang high among the branches. At a great distance we could hear the ringing, musical, bell-like note, long-drawn and of piercing sweetness, which occurs at intervals in the song; at first I thought this was the song, but when it was possible to approach the singer, I found that these far-sounding notes were scattered through a continuous song of great melody. I never listened to one that impressed me more.

from *Through the Brazilian Wilderness* (1914)

Herons Crying over the Black Lakes
J.M. SYNGE (1871–1909)

TRAMP [*At the door.*] Come along with me now, lady of the house, and it's not my blather you'll be hearing only, but you'll be hearing the herons crying out over the black lakes, and you'll be hearing the grouse and the owls with them, and the larks and the big thrushes when the days are warm, and it's not from the like of them you'll be hearing a talk of getting old like Peggy Cavanagh, and losing the hair off you, and the light of your eyes, but it's fine songs you'll be hearing when the sun goes up, and there'll be no old fellow wheezing, the like of a sick sheep, close to your ear.

from *In the Shadow of the Glen* (1904)

More Lovely in Voice than the Nightingale

BOYD ALEXANDER (1873–1910)

Four days more of this not very pleasant travelling brought us to the eastern end of the Kefl Sand Pandarange, the watershed of the Gurara and Kaduna rivers. … It was along these green-shaded watercourses and round the lily pools, in that enchanted hour at sunrise when Earth seems exhaling the fragrance of the just-departed fairies she has couched, and again when day pauses with drooped eyelids to catch the sound of night's soft foot-fall, I heard for the first time the entrancing song of the red thrush. More lovely in voice than the nightingale, more shy than she, his song seems the soaring spirit of the haunts in which he dwells; first, whispering notes like little puffs of wind through green leaves; then a soft soliloquy of liquid sounds like the stream that runs below his singing-bough, so sad that it is surely here beneath these waters that Narcissus lies. Quicker and louder mounts the song, to break in long notes that swoop and thrill with a passion that is all the sweet bird's own.

from *From the Niger to the Nile* (1907)

On the Horizons

D.H. LAWRENCE (1885–1930)

It seems when we hear a skylark singing as if sound were running forward into the future, running so fast and utterly without consideration, straight on into futurity. And when we hear a nightingale, we hear the pause and the rich, piercing rhythm of recollection, the perfect past. The lark may sound sad, but with the lovely lapsing sadness that is almost a swoon of hope. The nightingale's triumph is a pæan, but a death-pæan.

… Our birds sing on the horizons. They sing out of the blue, beyond us, or out of the quenched night. They sing at dawn and sunset. Only the poor, shrill, tame canaries whistle while we talk. The wild birds begin before we are awake, or as we drop into dimness, out of waking.

from Preface to *New Poems* (1920)

Greenshank

NORMAN MacCAIG (1910–1996)

His single note – one can't help calling it
piping, one can't help
calling it plaintive – slides droopingly down
no more than a semitone, but is filled
with an octave of loneliness, with the whole sad scale
of desolation.

He won't leave us. He keeps flying
fifty yards and perching
on a rock or a small hummock,
drawing attention to himself.
Then he calls and calls
and flies on again
in a flight
roundshouldered but dashing,
skulking yet bold.

Cuckoo, phoenix, nightingale,
you are no truer emblems
than this bird is.
He is the melancholy that flies
in the weathers of my mind,
He is the loneliness that calls to me there
in a semitone
of desolate octaves.

The Sky Lark's Soaring Song

KENN KAUFMAN (1954–)

It grew out of wave-noise and wind-sound, beginning
in low trilled notes, soft but clear, one following rapidly
on another. The sound arose from the fields somewhere
between me and the shoreline, and it was at once so
natural and so alien to the scene that it seemed to be a
song without a singer. These first notes were identical
in pitch, they did not ascend or descend the scale, but
the source of the voice seemed to be rising; too late it
occurred to me that the bird must be in the air. It was
singing as it flew straight upward. Then the invisible singer
seemed to reach a stationary peak in the sky, and the song
burst into a cascade of clear notes. The sound grew louder
and then softened again, broke into loud warbling passages
and then receded through quiet chirring trills; and the
song went on and on, without pause, from somewhere up
above.

With a start, I realized that I was standing open-
mouthed and staring at nothing. I began to look for the
singer – wanting reassurance that it was a bird, not imagi-
nation or the spirits of the island. My eyes strained against
the emptiness of the clouds.

There! So high above the earth that it was almost
beyond vision, the Sky Lark hovered on the wind.

from *Kingbird Highway: The Story of a Natural
Obsession that Got a Little Out of Hand* (2000)

The Dawn Chorus

BARBARA KINGSOLVER (1955–)

The other warblers woke up soon after the black-and-white: first she heard the syncopated phrase of the hooded warbler with its upbeat ending like a good joke, then the Kentucky with his more solemn, rolling trill. By now a faint gray light was seeping up the edge of the sky, or what she could see of the sky through the black-armed trees. This hollow was a mean divide, with mountains rising steeply on both sides and the trees towering higher still. The cabin was no place to be if you craved long days and sunlight, but there was no better dawn chorus anywhere on earth. In the high season of courtship and mating, this music was like the earth itself opening its mouth to sing. Its crescendo crept forward slowly as the daylight roused one bird and then another: the black-capped and Carolina chickadees came next, first cousins who whistled their notes on separate pitches, close together, distinguishable to any chickadee but to very few humans, especially among this choir of other voices. Deanna smiled to hear the first veery, whose song sounded like a thumb run down the tines of a comb. It had been the first birdcall to capture her fascination in childhood – not the calls of the meadowlarks and sparrows that sang outside her windows on the farm every morning, but the song of the veery, a high-elevation migrant that she encountered only up here, on fishing expeditions with her dad. Maybe she'd just never really listened before those trips, which yielded few trout and less conversation but so much silent waiting in the woods. ...

The dawn chorus was a whistling roar by now, the sound of a thousand males calling out love to a thousand silent females ready to choose and make the world new. It was nothing but heady cacophony unless you paid attention to the individual entries: a rose-breasted grosbeak with his sweet, complicated little sonnet; a vireo with his repetitious bursts of eighth notes and triplets. And then came the wood thrush, with his tone poem of a birdsong. The wood thrush defined these woods for Deanna, providing background music for her thoughts and naming her place in the forest. The dawn chorus would subside in another hour, but the wood thrush would persist for a long time into the morning, then pick up again in early evening or even at midday if it was cloudy. Nannie had asked her once in a letter how she could live up here alone with all the *quiet*, and that was Deanna's answer: when human conversation stopped, the world was anything but *quiet*. She lived with wood thrushes for company.

from *Prodigal Summer* (2001)

The Storm Petrels' Song

TIM DEE (1961–)

Storm petrel song is the strangest of music. The birds breed in tiny chinks between the stones of the broch, and from its curving wall came a squeaky skirl as if the stones were being rubbed together. A second petrel made a start-up burp a few feet away, and then another, though it was hard to tell where the sounds were coming from or to imagine how a bird was making them. I stood in the dark on the spiral stone stairs, listening to rock music inside a giant's ear.

All night birds' night songs sound ancient, weird and dark: the reels of grasshopper warblers, the grunts of woodcock, owl yelps, corncrake rasps, nightjar churrs, even the tearing-apart music of nightingales. They come up from a very old earth: the word chthonic manages to look how they sound as well as describing what they are. The storm petrels' song is even weirder: a furry pulse from the back of a tiny throat hidden in a crack of a rock. It is an inward and sibylline sound of swazzle notes and speaking stones. It giggles and rewinds. It clucks and purrs. It sounds like a simultaneous possession and exorcism. It is a noise reserved for the night and the deeper dark of the petrels' nesting holes. It would be unimaginable in daylight and inaudible over even the quietest of seas. It defines the deep contrariness of the midsummer storm petrel.

from *The Running Sky: A Birdwatching Life* (2009)

from *A Cock Crows in Rwanda*

Edouard Bamporiki (1983–)

Usually, beloved, I crow,
And my name is Rusake the Cock,
The same one most people chow down on,
Especially my delicious neck.
I'm at every wedding,
And on every chief's table,
Everyone likes me.
Let me come crow the story of Rwanda.
I witnessed bad times,
I travelled to many countries,
And in each I asked
Where the tragedy that decimates
The Rwandese came from.
Nations were watching.
Rusake, I'm sorrowful.

Can I ask you for a favour?
Protect me from insatiably hungry people.
I want to crow my troubles, first.
And then those who want to eat me may.
I know that if I leave,
If I leave this place without crowing my troubles,
You won't say anything about it,
You will just enjoy eating Rusake.

Then those that destroy my nation
Will be forgotten in Rwanda
Unless I crow about them,
So that we can remember their mistakes,
So that future generations will not poke me with
    their fingers.

trans. Arlette Maregeya and David Shook (2012)

A BIRDING YEAR
Summer

Loude Sing Cuckoo!

ANON

Sumer is icumen in,
Loude sing cuckou!
Groweth seed and bloweth meed,
And springth the wode now.
Sing cuckou!

Ewe bleteth after lamb,
Loweth after calve cow,
Bulloc sterteth, bucke verteth,
Merye sing cuckou!
Cuckou, cuckou,
Wel singest thou cuckou:
Ne swik thou never now!

This Temple-Haunting Martlet

WILLIAM SHAKESPEARE (1564–1616)

Before Macbeth's Castle

BANQUO   This guest of summer,
The temple-haunting martlet, does approve
By his loved mansionry that the heavens' breath
Smells wooingly here. No jutty, frieze,
Buttress, nor coign of vantage but this bird
Hath made his pendent bed and procreant cradle;
Where they most breed and haunt I have observed
The air is delicate.

from *Macbeth*

Our Summer Friends the Swallows

DANIEL DEFOE (1660–1731)

At this town in particular [Southwold], and so at all the
towns on this coast, from Orford-Ness to Yarmouth, is the
ordinary place where our summer friends the swallows, first
land when they come to visit us; and here they may be said
to embark for their return, when they go back into warmer
climates; and, as I think the following remark, tho' of so
trifling a circumstance, may be both instructing, as well as
diverting, it may be very proper in this place. The case is
this; I was some years before at this place, at the latter end of
the year (viz.) about the beginning of October, and lodging
in a house that looked into the church-yard, I observ'd in the
evening an unusual multitude of birds sitting on the leads of
the church; curiosity led me to go nearer to see what they
were, and I found they were all swallows; that there was
such an infinite number that they cover'd the whole roof of
the church, and of several houses near, and perhaps might,
of more houses which I did not see; this led me to enquire of
a grave gentleman whom I saw near me, what the meaning
was of such a prodigious multitude of swallows sitting there;
O Sir, says he, turning towards the sea, you may see the
reason, the wind is off sea. I did not seem fully informed by
that expression; so he goes on: I perceive, sir, says he, you
are a stranger to it; you must then understand first, that
this is the season of the year when the swallows, their food
here failing, begin to leave us, and return to the country,
where-ever it be, from whence I suppose they came; and this
being the nearest to the coast of Holland, they come here to
embark; this he said smiling a little; and now, sir, says he,

the weather being too calm, or the wind contrary, they are
waiting for a gale, for they are all wind-bound.

This was more evident to me, when in the morning I
found the wind had come about to the north-west in the
night, and there was not one swallow to be seen, of near a
million, which I believe was there the night before.

from *A Tour through the Whole Island of Great Britain* (1724–27)

The Naturalist's Summer-Evening Walk

GILBERT WHITE (1720–1793)

When day declining sheds a milder gleam,
What time the may-fly haunts the pool or stream;
When the still owl skims round the grassy mead,
What time the timorous hare limps forth to feed;
Then be the time to steal adown the vale,
And listen to the vagrant cuckoo's tale;
To hear the clamorous curlew call his mate,
Or the soft quail his tender pain relate;
To see the swallow sweep the dark'ning plain
Belated, to support her infant train;
To mark the swift in rapid giddy ring
Dash round the steeple, unsubdu'd of wing:
Amusive birds! – say where your hid retreat
When the frost rages and the tempests beat;
Whence your return, by such nice instinct led,
When spring, soft season, lifts her bloomy head?
Such baffled searches mock man's prying pride,
The God of Nature is your secret guide!
While deep'ning shades obscure the face of day

To yonder bench leaf-shelter'd let us stray,
'Till blended objects fail the swimming sight,
And all the fading landscape sinks in night;
To hear the drowsy dor come brushing by
With buzzing wing, or the shrill cricket cry;
To see the feeding bat glance through the wood;
To catch the distant falling of the flood;
While o'er the cliff th'awakened churn-owl hung
Through the still gloom protracts his chattering song;
While high in air, and pois'd upon his wings,
Unseen, the soft, enamour'd woodlark sings:
These, Nature's works, the curious mind employ,
Inspire a soothing melancholy joy

from *The Natural History of Selborne* (1789)

The Incumbent Linnet

ERASMUS DARWIN (1731–1802)

Now vows connubial chain the plighted pair,
And join paternal with maternal care;
The married birds with nice selection cull
Soft thistle-down, gray moss, and scattered wool,
Line the secluded nest with feathery rings,
Meet with fond bills, and woo with fluttering wings.
Week after week, regardless of her food,
The incumbent Linnet warms her future brood;
Each spotted egg with ivory lips she turns,
Day after day with fond expectance burns,
Hears the young prisoner chirping in his cell,
And breaks in hemispheres the obdurate shell.

from *The Temple of Nature* (1803)

Falling of the Swallow's Nest

DOROTHY WORDSWORTH (1771–1855)

Friday, 25th June [1802] … I went, just before tea, into
the garden. I looked up at my swallow's nest, and it was
gone. It had fallen down. Poor little creatures, they could
not themselves be more distressed than I was. I went
upstairs to look at the ruins. They lay in a large heap
upon the window ledge; these swallows had been ten days
employed in building this nest, and it seemed to be almost
finished. I had watched them early in the morning, in the
day many and many a time, and in the evenings when it
was almost dark. I had seen them sitting together side
by side in their unfinished nest, both morning and night.
When they first came about the window they used to
hang against the panes, with their white bellies and their
forked tails, looking like fish; but then they fluttered and
sang their own little twittering song. As soon as the nest
was broad enough, a sort of ledge for them, they sate both
mornings and evenings, but they did not pass the night
there. I watched them one morning, when William was
at Eusemere, for more than an hour. Every now and then
there was a motion in their wings, a sort of tremulousness,
and they sang a low song to one another.

… It is now eight o'clock; I will go and see if my
swallows are on their nest. Yes! there they are, side by
side, both looking down into the garden.

from Journals of Dorothy Wordsworth

The Swallow – one of my Favourite Birds

Humphry Davy (1778–1829)

Hal.—Whilst we have been conversing, the May-flies, which were in such quantities, have become much fewer; and I believe the reason is, that they have been greatly diminished by the flocks of swallows, which everywhere pursue them: I have seen a single swallow take four, in less than a quarter of a minute, that were descending to the water.

Poiet.—I delight in this living landscape! The swallow is one of my favourite birds, and a rival of the nightingale; for he cheers my sense of seeing as much as the other does my sense of hearing. He is the glad prophet of the year – the harbinger of the best season: he lives a life of enjoyment amongst the loveliest forms of nature: winter is unknown to him; and he leaves the green meadows of England in autumn, for the myrtle and orange groves of Italy, and for the palms of Africa:– he has always objects of pursuit, and his success is secure. Even the beings selected for his prey are poetical, beautiful, and transient. The ephemeræ are saved by his means from a slow and lingering death in the evening, and killed in a moment, when they have known nothing of life but pleasure. He is the constant destroyer of insects, – the friend of man; and, with the stork and the ibis, may be regarded as a sacred bird. His instinct, which gives him his appointed seasons, and teaches him always when and where to move, may be regarded as flowing from a Divine Source; and he belongs to the Oracles of Nature, which speak the awful and intelligible language of a present Deity.

from *Salmonia: Days of Fly Fishing* (1832)

The Thrush's Nest

JOHN CLARE (1793–1864)

Within a thick and spreading hawthorn bush
That overhung a molehill large and round,
I heard from morn to morn a merry thrush
Sing hymns to sunrise, and I drank the sound
With joy; and, often an intruding guest,
I watched her secret toil from day to day –
How true she warped the moss to form a nest,
And modelled it within the wood and clay;
And by and by, like heath-bells gilt with dew,
There lay her shining eggs, as bright as flowers,
Ink-spotted over shells of greeny blue;
And there I witnessed, in the sunny hours,
A brood of nature's minstrels chirp and fly,
Glad as that sunshine and the laughing sky.

The Pleasantest Manner of Spending a Hot July Day

EMILY BRONTË (1814–1848)

He said the pleasantest manner of spending a hot July
day was lying from morning till evening on a bank of
heath in the middle of the moors, with the bees humming
dreamily about among the bloom, and the larks singing
high up overhead, and the blue sky and bright sun shining
steadily and cloudlessly. That was his most perfect idea of
heaven's happiness: mine was rocking in a rustling green
tree, with a west wind blowing, and bright white clouds

flitting rapidly above; and not only larks, but throstles, and blackbirds, and linnets, and cuckoos pouring out music on every side, and the moors seen at a distance, broken into cool dusky dells; but close by great swells of long grass undulating in waves to the breeze; and woods and sounding water, and the whole world awake and wild with joy. He wanted all to lie in an ecstasy of peace; I wanted all to sparkle and dance in a glorious jubilee. I said his heaven would be only half alive …

from *Wuthering Heights* (1847)

The Heart of Summer
WILLIAM MORRIS (1834–1896)

My companion gave a sigh of pleased surprise and enjoyment; nor did I wonder, for the garden between the wall and the house was redolent of the June flowers, and the roses were rolling over one another with that delicious superabundance of small well-tended gardens which at first sight takes away all thought from the beholder save that of beauty. The blackbirds were singing their loudest, the doves were cooing on the roof-ridge, the rooks in the high elm-trees beyond were garrulous among the young leaves, and the swifts wheeled whining about the gables. And the house itself was a fit guardian for all the beauty of this heart of summer.

from *News from Nowhere* (1908)

Long-lived Summer Days

RICHARD JEFFERIES (1848–1887)

The long-lived summer days dried and warmed the turf
in the meadows. I used to lie down in solitary corners at
full length on my back, so as to feel the embrace of the
earth. The grass stood high above me, and the shadows of
the tree branches danced on my face. I looked up at the
sky, with half-closed eyes to bear the dazzling light. Bees
buzzed over me, sometimes a butterfly passed, there was a
hum in the air, green-finches sang in the hedge. Gradually
entering into the intense life of the summer days, – a
life which burned around as if every grass blade and leaf
were a torch, – I came to feel the long-drawn life of the
earth back into the dimmest past, while the sun of the
moment was warm on me. ... Dreamy in appearance, I
was breathing full of existence; I was aware of the grass-
blades, the flowers, the leaves on hawthorn and tree. I
seemed to live more largely through them, as if each were
a pore through which I drank. The grasshoppers called
and leaped, the green-finches sang, the blackbirds happily
fluted, all the air hummed with life. I was plunged deep in
existence, and with all that existence I prayed.

Through every grass-blade in the thousand thousand
grasses; through the million leaves, veined and edge-cut,
on bush and tree; through the song-notes and the marked
feathers of the birds; through the insects' hum and the
color of the butterflies; through the soft warm air, the
flecks of clouds dissolving, – I used them all for prayer...

from *The Story of My Heart* (1883)

Goldfinch Summer

RALPH HOFFMANN (1870–1932)

Not the most sullen sky nor the bitterest cold seems to discourage Goldfinches. They are always cheerful and affectionate, keeping together for the greater part of the year in larger or smaller flocks, which call to each other, if separated, by notes as sweet as those of a Canary. In summer, Goldfinches find an abundance of food in the seeds of many species of plants, but in winter also many remain even in the Northern States, searching cheerfully among the dry weeds and grasses, and uttering their sweet notes. Many people, however, do not notice them at this season, for when winter comes the head and body of the males of this species, as of many others, lose the bright black and yellow which marks them so distinctly in summer, and are clothed in dull brownish shades. About the first of April, one notices here and there in a flock a male that shows a few bright yellow feathers, and by another month, they have moulted their winter dress and are as gay as ever.

In the spring and early summer, the Goldfinches are extremely musical, spending hours in uttering a simple but pleasing song. Several males now engage in what seems to be a musical contest, flying out from a tree and circling about with set wings, all the time keeping up a continual strain. When flying through the air at a considerable height, they go in long curves, and utter during each undulation three or four simple notes. As they seem constantly to have business in one part or other of the country, the wave-like flight and characteristic notes become a common feature of the summer landscape.

Though the Goldfinches are here all winter, they delay nesting till very much later than the other resident birds; the Chickadees have their first brood already out in the world by the time the Goldfinches determine on building. The female is a modest-colored little body, as is often the case where the male is bright. The pair generally build in July, and choose some thick leafy tree, often a maple or poplar, and there, on a limb at a considerable height from the ground, construct a very neat nest, deep and cup-shaped, built of fine materials and lined with down from plants like the thistle. Here five or six bluish white eggs are laid, and when in another month the young Goldfinches begin to fly, it is at once evident from their sharp, insistent crying. As the calling of the young Orioles is a mark of late June, so the notes of the young Goldfinches become associated with August.

Goldfinches are very fond of the seeds of many kinds of composite flowers; they bite holes in unripe dandelion heads and take out the seeds; thistles are another favorite food, and a row of sunflowers planted in the garden will not fail to attract them. In winter, besides the seeds of weeds, they feed on birch seeds, scattering the scales over the snow, and they even pull out the seeds of the pitch pine, when the scales begin to loosen toward spring.

No bird has livelier, more cheerful ways than our Goldfinch, and none becomes a greater favorite. People are often at considerable pains to remove the dandelion plants from their lawns; if the gay flowers themselves do not repay one for their presence, many would certainly allow them to remain in order to have the pleasant spectacle, in summer, of a flock of yellow Goldfinches scattered about the grass and feeding on the seeds.

from *Bird Portraits* (1901)

A Bird's Anger

W.H. DAVIES (1871–1940)

A summer's morning that has but one voice;
    Five hundred stocks, like golden lovers, lean
Their heads together, in their quiet way,
    And but one bird sings, of a number seen.

It is the lark, that louder, louder sings,
    As though but this one thought possessed his mind:
'You silent robin, blackbird, thrush, and finch,
    I'll sing enough for all you lazy kind!'

And when I hear him at this daring task,
    'Peace, little bird,' I say, 'and take some rest;
Stop that wild, screaming fire of angry song,
    Before it makes a coffin of your nest.'

A Blackbird Singing

EDWARD THOMAS (1878–1917)

As I was leaving Wantage I heard a blackbird singing in a
garden beyond the church. This was near the middle of
August and a full month since I had last heard one. The
heat had dried up the birds' songs all much earlier than
usual, and now the rain of the last night seemed to be
reviving one. The song was perfect and as strange a thing
as last year's snow.

from *The Icknield Way* (1916)

Summer in English Fields and Woods

EDWARD THOMAS (1878–1917)

July 5

Last cry of the cuckoo.

Yellow-ammer yet sings.

Sparrows flocking in the unmown fields: as they rise
their combined wings sound like a horse shaking himself
in the meads.

Peewits flocking: in much the same numbers as will be
seen henceforward until March.

from *The Woodland Life* (1897)

How I Hanker after the Swallows!

W.N.P. BARBELLION (1889–1919)

July 26, 1917

… From my window I look out on a field with Beech
hedge down one side and beyond, tall trees – one showing
in outline exactly like the profile of a Beefeater's head,
more especially at sunset each evening when the tree
next behind is in shadow. The field is full of blue Scabious
plants, Wild Parsley and tall grass – getting brown now in
the sun. …

Then there are the Swallows and Martins cutting such
beautiful figures thro' the air that one wishes they carried
a pencil in their bills as they fly and traced the lines of
flight on a Bristol board. How I hanker after the Swallows!
so free and gay and vigorous. This autumn, as they prepare
to start, I shall hang on every twitter they make, and on
every wing-beat; and when they have gone, begin sadly to
set my house in order, as when some much loved visitors
have taken their departure. I am appreciating things a little
more the last few days.

from *The Journal of a Disappointed Man* (1919)

Summer for an Instant

George Orwell (1903–1950)

Summer-like for an instant the autumn sun bursts out,
And the light through the turning elms is green and clear;
It slants down the path and ragged marigolds glow
Fiery again, last flames of the dying year.

A blue-tit darts with a flash of wings, to feed
Where the coconut hangs on the pear tree over the well;
He digs at the meat like a tiny pickaxe tapping
With his needle-sharp beak as he clings to the swinging shell.

Then he runs up the trunk, sure-footed and sleek
   like a mouse,
And perches to sun himself; all his body and brain
Exult in the sudden sunlight, gladly believing
That the cold is over and summer is here again.

But I see the umber clouds that drive for the sun,
And a sorrow no argument ever can make away
Goes through my heart as I think of the nearing winter,
And the transient light that gleams like the ghost of May;

And the bird unaware, blessing the summer eternal,
Joyfully labouring, proud in his strength, gay-plumed,
Unaware of the hawk and the snow and the
   frost-bound nights,
And of his death foredoomed.

The Adelphi, May 1933

Summer's Coming In

Melissa Harrison (1975–)

Deep down the earth was still heavy with moisture, but
a few days' sun had dried the surface to a friable crust so
that it gave softly underfoot like half-baked sponge. Jack
set out, crossing the shallow ridges at an angle that made
stepping from one to another something he had to concentrate on, the gap between them not quite long enough
for his loping stride. In the warm soil around him flints
gleamed dully or glowed like bone. He knew of field edges,
elsewhere, that were piled high with them, the necessary
harvest of generations of children and women. And yet still
the earth sent them up.

   Above Jack red kites wheeled and tumbled into sudden
dogfights, and somewhere to his right the sun flashed
off the windscreens of the traffic on the Roman road.
A cuckoo called, and Jack froze, scalp prickling, until
the soft note came again, settling lazily over the field like
a pair of falling feathers. *Summer's coming in*, he thought,
turning a coin over in his pocket and grinning to himself.
It felt like a good omen.

from *At Hawthorn Time* (2015)

BIRDS *in* FLIGHT

from *Paradise Lost*

JOHN MILTON (1608–1674)

                    The eagle and the stork
On cliffs and cedar tops their eyries build:
Part loosely wing the region, part more wise
In common ranged in figure, wedge their way,
Intelligent of seasons, and set forth
Their aery caravan, high over seas
Flying, and over lands, with mutual wing
Easing their flight; so steers the prudent crane
Her annual voyage, borne on winds; the air
Floats as they pass, fanned with unnumbered plumes.
From branch to branch the smaller birds with song
Solaced the woods, and spread their painted wings
Till even; nor then the solemn nightingale
Ceased warbling, but all night tuned her soft lays.
Others on silver lakes and rivers bathed
Their downy breast; the swan, with arched neck
Between her white wings mantling proudly, rows
Her state with oary feet: yet oft they quit
The dank, and rising on stiff pennons tower
The mid aerial sky.

Birds in Flight

GILBERT WHITE (1720–1793)

Selborne, Aug. 7, 1778.
A good ornithologist should be able to distinguish birds
by their air as well as by their colours and shape; on the
ground as well as on the wing, and in the bush as well as
in the hand. ...

Thus kites and buzzards sail round in circles with wings
expanded and motionless; and it is from their gliding
manner that the former are still called in the north of
England gleads, from the Saxon verb *glidan* to glide. The
kestrel, or wind-hover, has a peculiar mode of hanging in
the air in one place, his wings all the while being briskly
agitated. Hen-harriers fly low over heaths or fields of corn,
and beat the ground regularly like a pointer or setting-dog.
Owls move in a buoyant manner, as if lighter than the air;
they seem to want ballast. There is a peculiarity belonging
to ravens that must draw the attention even of the most
incurious – they spend all their leisure time in striking
and cuffing each other on the wing in a kind of playful
skirmish; and, when they move from one place to another,
frequently turn on their backs with a loud croak, and seem
to be falling to the ground. When this odd gesture betides
them, they are scratching themselves with one foot, and
thus lose the centre of gravity. Rooks sometimes dive and
tumble in a frolicsome manner; crows and daws swagger
in their walk; woodpeckers fly *volatu undoso*, opening and
closing their wings at every stroke, and so are always rising
or falling in curves. All of this genus use their tails, which
incline downward, as a support while they run up trees.

Parrots, like all other hook-clawed birds, walk awkwardly, and make use of their bill as a third foot, climbing and ascending with ridiculous caution. All the *gallinae* parade and walk gracefully, and run nimbly; but fly with difficulty, with an impetuous whirring, and in a straight line. Magpies and jays flutter with powerless wings, and make no dispatch; herons seem incumbered with too much sail for their light bodies; but these vast hollow wings are necessary in carrying burdens, such as large fishes, and the like; pigeons, and particularly the sort called smiters, have a way of clashing their wings the one against the other over their backs with a loud snap; another variety called tumblers turn themselves over in the air. Some birds have movements peculiar to the season of love: thus ring-doves, though strong and rapid at other times, yet in the spring hang about on the wing in a toying and playful manner; thus the cock-snipe, while breeding, forgetting his former flight, fans the air like the wind-hover; and the greenfinch in particular exhibits such languishing and faltering gestures as to appear like a wounded and dying bird; the king-fisher darts along like an arrow; fern-owls, or goat-suckers, glance in the dusk over the tops of trees like a meteor; starlings as it were swim along, while missalthrushes use a wild and desultory flight; swallows sweep over the surface of the ground and water, and distinguish themselves by rapid turns and quick evolutions; swifts dash round in circles; and the bank-martin moves with frequent vacillations like a butterfly. Most of the small birds fly by jerks, rising and falling as they advance. Most small birds hop; but wagtails and larks walk, moving their legs alternately. Skylarks rise and fall perpendicularly as they sing:

woodlarks hang poised in the air; and titlarks rise and fall in large curves, singing in their descent. The white-throat uses odd jerks and gesticulations over the tops of hedges and bushes. All the duck-kind waddle; divers and auks walk as if fettered, and stand erect on their tails: these are the *compedes* of Linnaeus. Geese and cranes, and most wild-fowls, move in figured flights, often changing their position. The secondary remiges of *tringae*, wild-ducks, and some others, are very long, and give their wings, when in motion, an hooked appearance. Dab-chicks, moor-hens, and coots, fly erect, with their legs hanging down, and hardly make any dispatch; the reason is plain, their wings are placed too forward out of the true centre of gravity; as the legs of auks and divers are situated too backward.

from Letter to the Honourable Daines Barrington,
The Natural History of Selborne (1789)

The Jackdaw

WILLIAM COWPER (1731–1800)

There is a bird, who by his coat,
And by the hoarseness of his note,
Might be supposed a crow;
A great frequenter of the church,
Where, bishop-like, he finds a perch,
And dormitory too.

Above the steeple shines a plate,
That turns and turns, to indicate
From what point blows the weather:

Look up – your brains begin to swim,
'Tis in the clouds – that pleases him,
He chooses it the rather.

Fond of the speculative height,
Thither he wings his airy flight,
And thence securely sees
The bustle and the raree-show,
That occupy mankind below,
Secure and at his ease.

You think, no doubt, he sits and muses
On future broken bones and bruises,
If he should chance to fall.
No; not a single thought like that
Employs his philosophic pate,
Or troubles it at all.

He sees that this great roundabout –
The world, with all its motley rout,
Church, army, physic, law,
Its customs and its bus'nesses, –
Is no concern at all of his,
And says – what says he? – Caw.

Thrice happy bird! I too have seen
Much of the vanities of men;
And, sick of having seen 'em,
Would cheerfully these limbs resign
For such a pair of wings as thine,
And such a head between 'em.

To the Skylark

WILLIAM WORDSWORTH (1770–1850)

Ethereal minstrel! pilgrim of the sky!
Dost thou despise the earth where cares abound?
Or, while the wings aspire, are heart and eye
Both with thy nest upon the dewy ground?
Thy nest which thou canst drop into at will,
Those quivering wings composed, that music still!
Leave to the nightingale her shady wood;
A privacy of glorious light is thine;
Whence thou dost pour upon the world a flood
Of harmony, with instinct more divine;
Type of the wise who soar, but never roam;
True to the kindred points of heaven and home!

The Free Tenants of the Air

JAMES MONTGOMERY (1771–1854)

Flocking from every point of heaven, and filling
Eye, ear, and mind with objects, sounds, emotions
Akin to livelier sympathy and love
Than reptiles, fishes, insects could inspire;
– Birds, the free tenants of land, air, and ocean,
Their forms all symmetry, their motions grace;
In plumage, delicate and beautiful,
Thick without burthen, close as fishes' scales,
Or loose as full-blown poppies to the breeze;
With wings that might have had a soul within them,
They bore their owners by such sweet enchantment;

Birds, small and great, of endless shapes and colours,
Here flew and perched, there swam and dived at pleasure;
Watchful and agile, uttering voices wild
And harsh, yet in accordance with the waves
Upon the beach, the winds in caverns moaning,
Or winds and waves abroad upon the water.

from *Pelican Island* (1827)

The Ruby-Throated Humming Bird

JOHN JAMES AUDUBON (1785–1851)

No sooner has the returning sun again introduced the
vernal season, and caused millions of plants to expand their
leaves and blossoms to his genial beams, than the little
Humming Bird is seen advancing on fairy wings, carefully
visiting every opening flower-cup, and, like a curious florist,
removing from each the injurious insects that otherwise
would ere long cause their beauteous petals to droop and
decay. Poised in the air, it is observed peeping cautiously,
and with sparkling eye, into their innermost recesses, whilst
the etherial motions of its pinions, so rapid and so light,
appear to fan and cool the flower, without injuring its fragile
texture, and produce a delightful murmuring sound, well
adapted for lulling the insects to repose. Then is the moment
for the Humming Bird to secure them. Its long delicate bill
enters the cup of the flower, and the protruded double-tubed
tongue, delicately sensible, and imbued with a glutinous
saliva, touches each insect in succession, and draws it from
its lurking place, to be instantly swallowed. All this is done
in a moment, and the bird, as it leaves the flower, sips so

small a portion of its liquid honey, that the theft, we may suppose, is looked upon with a grateful feeling by the flower, which is thus kindly relieved from the attacks of her destroyers.

The prairies, the fields, the orchards and gardens, nay, the deepest shades of the forests, are all visited in their turn, and everywhere the little bird meets with pleasure and with food. Its gorgeous throat in beauty and brilliancy baffles all competition. Now it glows with a fiery hue, and again it is changed to the deepest velvety black. The upper parts of its delicate body are of resplendent changing green, and it throws itself through the air with a swiftness and vivacity hardly conceivable. It moves from one flower to another like a gleam of light, upwards, downwards, to the right, and to the left. In this manner, it searches the extreme northern portions of our country, following with great precaution the advances of the season, and retreats with equal care at the approach of autumn.

I wish it were in my power at this moment to impart to you, kind reader, the pleasures which I have felt whilst watching the movements, and viewing the manifestation of feelings displayed by a single pair of these most favourite little creatures, when engaged in the demonstration of their love to each other: – how the male swells his plumage and throat, and, dancing on the wing, whirls around the delicate female; how quickly he dives towards a flower, and returns with a loaded bill, which he offers to her to whom alone he feels desirous of being united; how full of ecstasy he seems to be when his caresses are kindly received; how his little wings fan her, as they fan the flowers, and he transfers to her bill the insect and the honey which he has procured with a view to please her; how these attentions are received with apparent satisfaction; how, soon after, the blissful compact is sealed; how, then, the courage and care of the male are redoubled; how he even dares to give chase to the Tyrant Fly-catcher, hurries the blue-Bird and the Martin to their boxes; and how, on sounding pinions, he joyously returns to the side of his lovely mate; Reader, all these proofs of the sincerity, fidelity, and courage, with which the male assures his mate of the care he will take of her while sitting on her nest, may be seen, and have been seen, but cannot be portrayed or described.

from *Birds of America* (1827–38)

from *To a Skylark*
PERCY BYSSHE SHELLEY (1792–1822)

Hail to thee, blithe Spirit!
    Bird thou never wert,
That from heaven or near it
    Pourest thy full heart
In profuse strains of unpremeditated art.

Higher still and higher
    From the earth thou springest
Like a cloud of fire;
    The blue deep thou wingest,
And singing still dost soar, and soaring ever singest.

In the golden lightning
    Of the sunken sun,
O'er which clouds are brightning,
    Thou dost float and run,
Like an unbodied joy whose race is just begun.

The pale purple even
   Melts around thy flight;
Like a star of heaven,
   In the broad daylight
Thou art unseen, but yet I hear thy shrill delight,

   Keen as are the arrows
     Of that silver sphere,
   Whose intense lamp narrows
     In the white dawn clear,
Until we hardly see, we feel that it is there.
. . .

   Better than all measures
     Of delightful sound,
   Better than all treasures
     That in books are found,
Thy skill to poet were, thou scorner of the ground!

   Teach me half the gladness
     That thy brain must know,
   Such harmonious madness
     From my lips would flow,
The world should listen then, as I am listening now!

The Flight of the Condor
CHARLES DARWIN (1809–1882)

April 27th [1834] – When the condors are wheeling in a
flock round and round any spot, their flight is beautiful.
Except when rising from the ground, I do not recollect

ever having seen one of these birds flap its wings. Near Lima, I watched several for nearly half an hour, without once taking off my eyes, they moved in large curves, sweeping in circles, descending and ascending without giving a single flap. As they glided close over my head, I intently watched from an oblique position, the outlines of the separate and great terminal feathers of each wing; and these separate feathers, if there had been the least vibratory movement, would have appeared as if blended together; but they were seen distinct against the blue sky. The head and neck were moved frequently, and apparently with force; and the extended wings seemed to form the fulcrum on which the movements of the neck, body, and tail acted. If the bird wished to descend, the wings were for a moment collapsed; and when again expanded with an altered inclination, the momentum gained by the rapid descent seemed to urge the bird upwards with the even and steady movement of a paper kite. In the case of any bird soaring, its motion must be sufficiently rapid so that the action of the inclined surface of its body on the atmosphere may counterbalance its gravity. The force to keep up the momentum of a body moving in a horizontal plane in the air (in which there is so little friction) cannot be great, and this force is all that is wanted. The movements of the neck and body of the condor, we must suppose, is sufficient for this. However this may be, it is truly wonderful and beautiful to see so great a bird, hour after hour, without any apparent exertion, wheeling and gliding over mountain and river.

from *The Voyage of the Beagle* (1839)

The Windhover

GERARD MANLEY HOPKINS (1844–1889)

To Christ Our Lord

I caught this morning morning's minion, king-
   dom of daylight's dauphin, dapple-dawn-drawn Falcon, in his riding
   Of the rolling level underneath him steady air, and striding
High there, how he rung upon the rein of a wimpling wing
In his ecstasy! then off, off forth on swing,
   As a skate's heel sweeps smooth on a bow-bend: the hurl and gliding
   Rebuffed the big wind. My heart in hiding
Stirred for a bird, – the achieve of, the mastery of the thing.

Brute beauty and valour and act, oh, air, pride, plume, here
   Buckle! AND the fire that breaks from thee then, a billion
Times told lovelier, more dangerous, O my chevalier!

   No wonder of it: shéer plód makes plough down sillion
Shine, and blue-bleak embers, ah my dear,
   Fall, gall themselves, and gash gold-vermilion.

The Cranes

ANTON CHEKHOV (1860–1904)

TUZENBACH Not only after two or three centuries, but in a million years, life will still be as it was; life does not change, it remains for ever, following its own laws which do not concern us, or which, at any rate, you will never find out. Migrant birds, cranes for example, fly and fly, and whatever thoughts, high or low, enter their heads, they will still fly and not know why or where. They fly and will continue to fly, whatever philosophers come to life among them; they may philosophize as much as they like, only they will fly...

from *The Three Sisters* (1901)

Night Hawks over Chicago

JOSEPH LANE HANCOCK (1864–1925)

Sailing here or abruptly tumbling in the air, the strange-winged form appears as a seeming spectre before our eyes. In the fall of the year we are forewarned of the first mysterious flight of the night hawk by the straggling advanced sentinel's rasping ze-e-e-e-t, as the sound comes in at the open window. ...

On the last day of August, 1902, at about five o'clock p.m., I noticed a flight of night hawks going south. From the porch of our home in Chicago I watched their flight as they came scattered along restlessly pursuing their way. The open view from where I stood would allow a vision of about a one-mile stretch, looking east.

At 5.26 p.m. I took note with watch in hand and counted all the individual twilight birds that passed the line of vision. In four minutes one hundred had passed the line, the time then being five-thirty. In another three and a half minutes one hundred more passed; the time now being five thirty-three and a half. Still continuing counting, another hundred birds passed just at 5.37 p.m., or in four minutes.

If this was a fair computation, one thousand five hundred birds would pass in an hour. Allowing only six miles as the width of the city, nine thousand birds would pass over the line drawn across the city at a given point in an hour. As a matter of fact, the birds fly in scattered flocks over a large area, and while these flocks come periodically, lasting into the night, there are quiescent spells when almost no birds are seen in the sky for a space of a minute to several minutes at a time. A fair estimate would indicate that eighteen thousand birds pass over the city in a single night in this migration the last of August.

from Nature Sketches in Temperate America (1911)

from *The Silver Gull*

JOHN LE GAY BRERETON (1871–1933)

With strong slow stroke
Oaring her way against the breeze
Above the blustering waves that shoulder and smoke
The silver gull moves on with strenuous ease;
Then sidelong shoots on high
With sudden cry
Of rapture in the wind's imperious will

And that sweet whirling dream
Of blending purpose;
Poised a moment, still,
She glides, a fancied shape of air, down that invisible
    stream.

I lie on the warm sea-beach
And out to the wandering heart
Of feathered life in the beating air I reach
Arms that beseech
– Arms of my soul that in the living air
As answer to my prayer
Are wings of ecstasy;
And on the fierce quest silently I start
Above the envious crowding of the sea.

The Flight of the Goldfinch

FREDERICK PHILIP GROVE (1879–1948)

And as if to make my enjoyment of the evening's drive
supreme, I saw the first flocks of my favourite bird,
the goldfinch. All over this vast expanse, which many
would have called a waste, there were strings of them,
chasing each other in their wavy flight, twittering on the
downward stretch, darting in among the bushes, turning
with incredible swiftness and sureness of wing the shortest
of curves about a branch, and undulating away again to
where they came from.

from *Over Prairie Trails* (1922)

Bird after Bird

James Joyce (1882–1941)

What birds were they? He stood on the steps of the library
to look at them, leaning wearily on his ashplant. They
flew round and round the jutting shoulder of a house in
Molesworth Street. The air of the late March evening
made clear their flight, their dark darting quivering bodies
flying clearly against the sky as against a limp-hung cloth of
smoky tenuous blue.

He watched their flight; bird after bird: a dark flash, a
swerve, a flutter of wings. He tried to count them before
all their darting quivering bodies passed: six, ten, eleven:
and wondered were they odd or even in number. Twelve,
thirteen: for two came wheeling down from the upper sky.
They were flying high and low but ever round and round in
straight and curving lines and ever flying from left to right,
circling about a temple of air.

He listened to the cries: like the squeak of mice behind
the wainscot: a shrill twofold note. But the notes were long
and shrill and whirring, unlike the cry of vermin, falling
a third or a fourth and trilled as the flying beaks clove the
air. Their cry was shrill and clear and fine and falling like
threads of silken light unwound from whirring spools.

The inhuman clamour soothed his ears in which his
mother's sobs and reproaches murmured insistently and
the dark frail quivering bodies wheeling and fluttering and
swerving round an airy temple of the tenuous sky soothed
his eyes which still saw the image of his mother's face.

Why was he gazing upwards from the steps of the porch,
hearing their shrill twofold cry, watching their flight? For

an augury of good or evil? A phrase of Cornelius Agrippa flew through his mind and then there flew hither and thither shapeless thoughts from Swedenborg on the correspondence of birds to things of the intellect and of how the creatures of the air have their knowledge and know their times and seasons because they, unlike man, are in the order of their life and have not perverted that order by reason. ...

They came back with shrill cries over the jutting shoulder of the house, flying darkly against the fading air. What birds were they? He thought that they must be swallows who had come back from the south. Then he was to go away for they were birds ever going and coming, building ever an unlasting home under the eaves of men's houses and ever leaving the homes they had built to wander.

from *A Portrait of the Artist as a Young Man* (1916)

One Gull-Day

H.J. MASSINGHAM (1888–1952)

I remember one gull-day in particular. The commonest species along the coast was the lesser blackback (though the herring ran it close), and they were always wandering on yellow legs over the grass and mud or flying over one's head uttering at intervals their gruff, hoarse *owk owk*, or *hah hah*, like the muttering of the wilderness. On this festival day there were gathered some four hundred or so birds, resting on the mud and facing one another in two long lines. The blackbacks were greatly in the majority and were all facing one way, head to wind, as is usual with gulls, and in the manner of lapwings and fieldfares, producing a strong effect in their alternating blacks and whites. Then one great mass rose up, as it seemed, and possibly was, by telepathic suggestion, by a sudden rushing wind of common impulse, made a half-circle and joined forces with the other, creating such a confusion that the whole multitude was lifted ponderously up, and out of the cloud came threading the herring gulls like strands pulled out of a skein, their silver-grey wings gleaming in the level rays of the sun, and leaving the black volume to come foundering down again upon the yellow sand. Why the two species thus separated I cannot pretend to guess, but enough for me were the power and grandeur of the spectacle.

from *Some Birds of the Countryside: The Art of Nature* (1921)

Mallard

REX WARNER (1905–1986)

Squawking they rise from reeds into the sun,
climbing like furies, running on blood and bone,
with wings like garden-shears clipping the misty air,
four mallard, hard-winged, with necks like rods
fly in perfect formation over the marsh.

Keeping their distance, gyring, not letting slip the air,
but leaping into it straight like hounds or divers,
they stretch out into the wind and sound their horns again.

Suddenly siding to a bank of air unbidden
by hand signal or morse message of command
downsky they plane, sliding like corks on a current,
designed so deftly that all air is advantage,

till, with few flaps, orderly as they left earth,
alighting among curlew they pad on mud.

Birds behind birds behind birds...

TIM DEE (1961–)

From all sides there were lines of starlings, in layers of
about fifteen birds thick stretching for three miles back
into the sky and coming towards the reed beds that surrounded me. They came out of the furthest reaches of the
air, materialising into it from beyond where my eyes or
binoculars could reach in the murk. All flew with a lightly
rippling glide, as if the net they were making of themselves
was being evenly drawn into a single point in the reed bed.

Their arrival and accumulation had been eerily silent.
From the early afternoon, first in the villages and then in
the staging fields, there had been great noise. A collective
telling and retelling of starling life rose through those hours
of pre-roost talk to a complicated but loquacious rendering
of all things – idiomatic adventure, mimetic brilliance and
delighted conversational murmur. Once this annotation of
the day was done, the birds grew quiet and lifted up and off
to begin their thickening flights towards the roost.

There were thousands of mute birds around me, their
wheeze and jabber left behind. Many thousands more were

too far away to hear, but their calm progress towards the roost suggested they flew in silence. Closer, the only noise was of the flock's feathers. As they wheeled and gyred en masse, the sound of their wings turning swept like brushes dashed across a snare drum or a Spanish fan being flicked open. The air was thick with starlings, inches apart and racked back into the darkening sky for a mile. Every bird was within a wing stretch of another. None touched.

A rougher magic overtook them as they arrived above the reeds. Great ductile cartwheels of birds were unleashed across the sky. Conjured balls of starlings rolled out and up, shoaling from their descending lines, thickening and pulling in on themselves – a black bloom burst from the seedbed of birds. One wheel hit another and the carousels of birds chimed and merged, like iron filings made to bend to a magnet. The flock – but *flock* doesn't say anything like enough – pulsed in and out.

from *The Running Sky: A Birdwatching Life* (2009)

The Gannetry

KATHLEEN JAMIE (1962–)

The colony was obvious: half a mile ahead, a column of birds turned bright and white in the summer air. They were visible as a loose plume as we walked over the island toward them, and doubtless visible for miles out to sea. It was exciting, like a fun fair; the closer we got to the cliff edge the more we could hear the racket, the more the breeze brought us the smell.

The cliffs were south-facing, full in the sun, and five hundred foot high. They formed promontories and bowls, so we walked out onto the broadest promontory and from there looked back into the cauldron the birds had commandeered for themselves. All was squalor and noise: the birds' tenement was so plastered with guano that it shone, and the airborne birds cast winged shadows on the whitewashed walls. Under these soothing shadows thousands more gannets were installed all along the cliff's ledges, tier above tier. The flying birds were perfectly silent. Those on the cliff, though, made a loud fretful noise. They were caught up in constant greetings, and constant disputes: about each other, about thefts and incursions, about the indignity of it all – the one demand the empty future makes of them: breed! breed! …

Just off the cliff edge, a few yards away from where we sat, gannet after gannet beat by, with outstretched beaks and hard eyes, taking the corner into the colony at speed, as if bearing urgent dispatches. We were close enough to see their eyes, and they are sharp-sighted, but if they noticed us they made no sign. We were nothing, land things, and gannets disdain land. They disdain land, but every spring they're lured to their traditional cliffs and stacks by a siren song. Never a summer that isn't spent like this, in fuss and bother, each pair raising a single chick.

from *Sightlines* (2012)

HAWKS
& EAGLES

The Eagle,
which hath principality among fowls

BARTHOLOMEUS ANGLICUS (*fl. c.* 1220–40)

Now it pertaineth to speak of birds and fowls, and in particular
and first of the eagle, which hath principality among fowls.
Among all manner kinds of divers fowls, the eagle is the more
liberal and free of heart. For the prey that she taketh, but it
be for great hunger, she eateth not alone, but putteth it forth
in common to fowls that follow her. But first she taketh her
own portion and part. And therefore oft other fowls follow
the eagle for hope and trust to have some part of her prey. But
when the prey that is taken is not sufficient to herself, then as
a king that taketh heed to a community, she taketh the bird
that is next to her, and giveth it among the others, and serveth
them therewith.

Austin saith, and Plinius also, that in age the eagle hath
darkness and dimness in eyen, and heaviness in wings. And
against this disadvantage she is taught by kind to seek a well
of springing water, and then she flieth up into the air as far as
she may, till she be full hot by heat of the air, and by travail of
flight, and so then by heat the pores are opened and the feathers
chafed, and she falleth suddenly in to the well, and there the
feathers are changed, and the dimness of her eyes is wiped away
and purged, and she taketh again her might and strength.

The eagle's feathers done and set among feathers of wings of
other birds corrupteth and fretteth them. As strings made of
wolf-gut done and put into a lute or in an harp among strings
made of sheep-gut do destroy, and fret, and corrupt the strings
made of sheep-gut, if it so be that they be set among them, as
in a lute or in an harp, as Pliny saith.

Among all fowls, in the eagle the virtue of sight is most mighty and strong. For in the eagle the spirit of sight is most temperate and most sharp in act and deed of seeing and beholding the sun in the roundness of its circle without blemishing of eyen. And the sharpness of her sight is not rebounded again with clearness of light of the sun, nother disperpled. There is one manner eagle that is full sharp of sight, and she taketh her own birds in her claws, and maketh them to look even on the sun, and that ere their wings be full grown, and except they look stiffly and steadfastly against the sun, she beateth them, and setteth them even tofore the sun. And if any eye of any of her birds watereth in looking on the sun she slayeth him, as though he went out of kind, or else driveth him out of the nest and despiseth him, and setteth not by him.

from *Mediaeval Lore from Bartholomew Anglicus*, ed. Robert Steele (1905)

The Falconer

MICHAEL DRAYTON (1563–1631)

When making for the brook, the falconer doth espy,
On river, plash, or mere, where store of fowl doth lie,
Whence forced over land, by skilful falconers' trade,
A faire convenient flight, may easily be made,
He whistleth off his hawks, whose nimble pinions straight,
Do work themselves by turns, into a stately height.
And if that after check, the one or both do go,
Sometimes he them the lure, sometimes doth water show;
The trembling fowl that hear the jigging hawk-bells ring,
And find it is too late, to trust them to their wing,

Lie flat upon the flood, whilst the high-mounted hawks,
Then being lords alone, in their etherial walks,
Aloft so bravely stir, their bells so thick that shake,
Which when the Falconer sees, that scarce one plane
   they make;
The gallant'st birds, said he, that ever flew on wing,
And swears there is a flight, were worthy of a king.

Then making to the flood, to cause the fowls to rise.
The fierce and eager hawks, down thrilling from the skies,
Make sundry canceleers e'er they the fowl can reach,
Which then to save their lives, their wings do lively stretch.
But when the whizzing bells the silent air do cleave,
And that their greatest speed, them vainly do deceive;
And the sharp cruel hawks, they at their backs do view,
Themselves for very fear they instantly ineaw.

The hawks get up again into their former place,
And ranging here and there, in that the airy race;
Still as the fearful fowl attempt to 'scape away,
With many a stoping brave, them in again they lay.
But when the falconers take their hawking-poles in hand,
And crossing of the brook, do put it over land;
The hawk gives it a souse, that makes it to rebound;
Well near the height of man, sometimes, above the ground;
Oft takes a leg, or wing, oft takes away the head,
And oft from neck to tail, the back in two doth shread.
With many a wo ho ho, and jocond lure again,
When he his quarry makes upon the grassy plain.

from *Polyolbion* (1612–22)

from *The Falcon*

RICHARD LOVELACE (1618–c. 1657)

Fair Princesse of the spacious Air,
That hast vouchsaf'd acquaintance here,
With us are quarter'd below stairs,
That can reach Heav'n with nought but Pray'rs;
Who, when our activ'st wings we try,
Advance a foot into the Sky.

Bright Heir t' th' Bird Imperial,
From whose avenging penons fall
Thunder and Lightning twisted Spun;
Brave Cousin-german to the Sun,
That didst forsake thy Throne and Sphere,
To be an humble Pris'ner here;
And for a pirch of her soft hand,
Resign the Royal Woods command.

How often would'st thou shoot Heav'ns Ark,
Then mount thy self into a Lark;
And after our short faint eyes call,
When now a Fly, now nought at all;
Then stoop so swift unto our Sence,
As thou wert sent Intelligence.
…
The Lanner and the Lanneret
Thy Colours bear as Banneret;
The Goshawk and her Tercel rows'd
With tears attend thee as new bows'd,

All these are in their dark array,
Led by the various Herald-jay.

But thy eternal name shall live
Whilst Quills from Ashes fame reprieve,
Whilst open stands renown's wide dore,
And Wings are left on which to soar;
Doctor Robbin, the prelate Pye,
And the poetick Swan shall dye,
Only to sing thy Elegie.

The Eagle and the Weasel

OLIVER GOLDSMITH (1728–1774)

The following story is told in Selkirkshire:–

'A group of haymakers, while busy at their work on
Chapelhope meadow, at the upper end of St. Mary's Loch
(or rather of the Loch of the Lowes, which is separated
from it by a narrow neck of land), saw an eagle rising
above the steep mountains that enclose the narrow valley.
The eagle himself was, indeed, no unusual sight; but there
is something so imposing and majestic in the flight of this
noble bird, while he soars upwards in spiral circles, that it
fascinates the attention of most people. But the spectators
were soon aware of something peculiar in the flight of the
bird they were observing. He used his wings violently, and
the strokes were often repeated, as if he had been alarmed
and hurried by unusual agitation; and they noticed, at
the same time, that he wheeled in circles that seemed
constantly decreasing, while his ascent was proportionally

rapid. The now idle haymakers drew together in close consultation on the singular case, and continued to keep their eyes on the seemingly distressed eagle, until he was nearly out of sight, rising still higher and higher into the air. In a short while, however, they were all convinced that he was again seeking the earth, evidently not as he ascended, in spiral curves; it was like something falling, and with great rapidity. But, as he approached the ground, they clearly saw he was tumbling in his fall like a shot bird; the convulsive fluttering of his powerful wings stopping the descent but very little, until he fell at a small distance from the men and boys of the party, who had naturally run forward, highly excited by the strange occurrence. A large black-tailed weasel or stoat ran from the body as they came near, turned with the usual *nonchalance* and impudence of the tribe, stood up on its hind legs, crossed its forepaws over its nose, and surveyed its enemies a moment or two (as they often do when no dog is near), and bounded into a saugh bush. The king of the air was dead; and, what was more surprising, he was covered with his own blood; and, upon further examination, they found his throat cut, and the stoat has been suspected as the regicide unto this day.'

from *Natural History* (1763)

Young Eagles Take Flight

HUMPHRY DAVY (1778–1829)

I once saw a very fine and interesting sight above one of the
Crags of Ben Weevis, near Strathgarve, as I was going, on
the 20th of August, in pursuit of black game. Two parent
eagles were teaching their offspring – two young birds, the
manœuvres of flight. They began by rising from the top of
a mountain in the eye of the sun (it was about midday, and
bright for this climate). They at first made small circles,
and the young birds imitated them; they paused on their
wings, waiting till they had made their first flight, and then
took a second and larger gyration, – always rising towards
the sun, and enlarging their circle of flight so as to make
a gradually extending spiral. The young ones still slowly
followed, apparently flying better as they mounted; and
they continued this sublime kind of exercise, always rising,
till they became mere points in the air, and the young
ones were lost, and afterwards their parents, to our aching
sight.

from *Salmonia: Days of Fly Fishing* (1832)

The Hawk and the Lark

WILLIAM MACGILLIVRAY (1796–1852)

When about a mile beyond the Loch of Achlossan, I had
my attention attracted by the cries of a Lark, which I
saw pursued by a Hawk. It strove incessantly to keep
above its enemy, which equally endeavoured to gain the
ascendancy, and sometimes succeeded. Numerous were the

attempts the Hawk made to seize the little bird, which, with wonderful agility, always evaded it by turning aside and shooting abruptly upwards. A single false movement would have been fatal. The Hawk, unable to turn so quickly as the Lark, endeavoured to seize it from one side, then from the other, sometimes from beneath, and now and then from above. Whenever it attempted to ascend, the Lark strove to outdo it, and frequently succeeded. It seemed as if the Lark could not venture to shoot off, for it always kept close to the Hawk. The chase continued about fifteen minutes, attempts at seizure being made at very short intervals all that time. Sometimes the Hawk, shooting down obliquely, the Lark however evading it, could not overcome the impetus given in time to have another clutch, but wheeled off to some distance. At length the Lark appeared almost exhausted, and seemed drawing near the end of its career. Unable to rise above its enemy, and coming nearer and nearer to the ground, it tried a rapid descent, but was instantly overtaken, and repeatedly pounced at. The birds were now for a while quite close to each other, and several very quick movements were made by the Hawk, and dexterously avoided by the Lark. They were gradually descending, when the Lark suddenly sped away towards a farm-steading about five hundred yards distant. The Hawk pursued, and both passed so near to me, as I leaned against a wall, that the grayish-blue tint of the dorsal plumage, and the black moustaches of the pursuer were distinctly visible. Rapidly shooting in between the corn-stacks, the Lark was as rapidly followed. In a little while both birds reappeared, flew round the house, and amongst the trees in the garden, then again shot in between the stacks, darted back among the trees, rose high above them, and then sped away to this side and that, the Lark all the while emitting at short intervals a low chirp, the Hawk silent. At length, the Lark suddenly dropped down among the trees and into the bushes, but so did the Hawk. It was all over I thought; but no – when the Hawk reappeared, he had nothing in his talons. He flew slowly along one side of the garden wall, then along the other, shot in among the trees, then among the stacks, flew round the house, searched the trees once more; but not finding what he looked for, flew off to a small tree by the road, and alighted on it.

from *The Natural History of Dee Side and Braemar* (1855)

The Eagle

ALFRED, LORD TENNYSON (1809–1892)

He clasps the crag with crookèd hands;
Close to the sun in lonely lands,
Ring'd with the azure world, he stands.

The wrinkled sea beneath him crawls;
He watches from his mountain walls,
And like a thunderbolt he falls.

The Fish-Hawk and the Pelican

DAVID LIVINGSTONE (1813–1873)

This fish-hawk generally kills more prey than it can devour.
It eats a portion of the back of the fish, and leaves the rest
for the Barotse, who often had a race across the river when
they saw an abandoned morsel lying on the opposite sand-
banks. The hawk is, however, not always so generous, for, as
I myself was a witness on the Zouga, it sometimes plunders
the purse of the pelican. Soaring overhead, and seeing this
large, stupid bird fishing beneath, it watches till a fine fish
is safe in the pelican's pouch; then descending, not very
quickly, but with considerable noise of wing, the pelican
looks up to see what is the matter, and, as the hawk comes
near, he supposes that he is about to be killed, and roars out
'Murder!' The opening of his mouth enables the hawk to
whisk the fish out of the pouch, upon which the pelican does
not fly away, but commences fishing again, the fright having
probably made him forget he had anything in his purse.

from *Missionary Travels and Researches in South Africa* (1857)

The Dalliance of the Eagles

WALT WHITMAN (1819–1892)

Skirting the river road, (my forenoon walk, my rest,)
Skyward in air a sudden muffled sound, the dalliance of the
    eagles,
The rushing amorous contact high in space together,
The clinching interlocking claws, a living, fierce, gyrating
    wheel,
Four beating wings, two beaks, a swirling mass tight
    grappling,
In tumbling turning clustering loops, straight downward
    falling,
Till o'er the river pois'd, the twain yet one, a moment's lull,
A motionless still balance in the air, then parting, talons
    loosing,
Upward again on slow-firm pinions slanting, their separate
    diverse flight,
She hers, he his, pursuing.

Hawking in the Arabian Desert

H.B. TRISTRAM (1822–1906)

No agha or sheik of high degree ever moves for war,
pleasure, or business unattended by his falconers, who are
his confidential lieutenants. The care of three falcons is
considered sufficient employment for one falconer with an
assistant; and on the march one or two of these important
personages follow mounted immediately behind the sheik,
with a hooded falcon on the wrist, one on the shoulder,
and another on the top of his head. The houbara bustard is
the favourite quarry, but eagles, kites, sandgrouse (and, in
the case of the large sakk'r falcon, the gazelle), afford equal
sport to the huntsman.

Our day's pursuit was to be the bustard. When one is
descried the whole cavalcade instantly halt; the hawk on
the wrist is transferred to the hand of his master, who,
attended by the favoured few, instantly sets off, and,
unhooding his bird, throws him towards the bustard.
Much skill is exercised in drawing the attention of the
falcon to the game before it rises. Should it unfortunately
take wing before its pursuer has poised herself above it, an
ill-trained or impetuous bird is very apt to strike it in the
air; this, according to the view of your desert connoisseur,
is a most impardonable and unsportsmanlike offence, to
be punished with death. A skilful hawk will at once rise
to a considerable height; then swooping down, make feints
till the bustard takes to its legs instead of its wings. The
falcon then poises herself over it, while a second is flung
off the wrist, and the two together give chase, the speed of
the houbara being such that a fleet Arab horse can scarcely

keep up with the pursuit. The poor bird runs along, aiding its speed by a perpetual fanning with its wings, its head stretched forward like a corncrake's, and its conspicuous black and white ruff folded close over its neck, a pitiable contrast to the proud fellow who was lately sitting with head erect, elevated crest, and expanded ruff, challenging all comers. The pursuers hang over him at the height of only a few yards, and at each effort he makes to take wing swoop down with a feint. It is considered the excellency of a falcon to make these feints at the quarry till he is nearly exhausted, when the fatal swoop is made, and the bird instantly drops, struck dead by the hind claw having pierced its vertebrae.

from *The Great Sahara: Wanderings South of the Atlas Mountains* (1860)

Choosing a Hawk

James Edmund Harting (1841–1928)

For a beginner I would certainly recommend a Merlin. No hawk so soon becomes tame, or is more easily trained, and, at the same time, is less liable to be lost. An eyess tiercel, however – that is a male Peregrine taken from the nest – is almost as tractable, and, if properly handled, will become tame in an incredibly short time, manifesting a docility which, to persons knowing about hawks, is very surprising. Sparrowhawks and Goshawks need rather more skill in handling, requiring to be carried a great deal, and have at first a troublesome habit of 'bating off', or flying from the hand, every few minutes, hanging head downwards by the jesses, and required to be gently and adroitly replaced with a frequency which is very trying to the patience of the owner. On this account I would say to the tyro, begin with a Merlin, or eyess Peregrine....

When choosing a hawk, see that the eyes are full and bright: sunken eyes and contracted pupils are a sure indication of ill-health. The tongue and inside of the mouth should be pink: a furred tongue of a whitey-brown colour is a bad sign. The head should be flat, the shoulders broad, the wings long and well crossed over the tail when closed. The pectoral muscles (under the wing) should be full and firm to the touch, not soft and flabby. The flight feathers should be perfect (ten in each wing), and should have good broad webs. It is easy to examine them after hooding the bird by gently expanding each wing by turn. The thighs should be muscular, the feet large and strong.

from *Hints on the Management of Hawks* (1898)

Falconry in India

Douglas Dewar (1875–1957)

The month is December, and the place Oudh. This means a sunny but perfectly cool day, so that riding, even when the sun is at its zenith, is delightful. Our party consists of an Indian gentleman – a Sikh and a large landholder – who owns the hawks, and three Europeans all well mounted, also the chief falconer, indifferently mounted, who carries on his gloved forearm a goshawk. ...

[P]resently [we] come to a narrow river running through a deep *nullah*. Here two or three cormorants come flying

overhead. They are forthwith 'spotted' by the goshawks,
which have all the time been eagerly looking about them
in all directions. Having seen the cormorants, they begin
tugging excitedly at their jesses. The falconers liberate the
goshawks, and away they go in pursuit. After flying about
eighty yards, first one goshawk, then the other, gives up
the chase, and each repairs to the tree that happens to be
nearest it. Then the falconers go up and show the birds
pieces of meat, in order to entice them back to the fist.
One *baz* immediately flies to the bait. Not so the other.
She sits perched in her tree with an air of *j'y suis, j'y reste*.
In a few seconds some crows catch sight of her and proceed
to mob her by flying around her and squawking loudly.
However, not one of them dares to touch her. Presently she
too flies to her trainer, and the party moves on.

from *Indian Natural History Sketches* (1912)

The Buzzards

MARTIN ARMSTRONG (1882–1974)

When evening came and the warm glow grew deeper,
And every tree that bordered the green meadows
    And in the yellow cornfields every reaper
And every corn-shock stood above their shadows
Flung eastward from their feet in longer measure,
Serenely far there swam in the sunny height
A buzzard and his mate who took their pleasure
Swirling and poising idly in golden light.

On great pied motionless moth-wings borne along,
    So effortless and so strong,
Cutting each other's paths, together they glided,
Then wheeled asunder till they soared divided
Two valleys' width (as though it were delight
To part like this, being sure they could unite
So swiftly in their empty, free dominion),
Curved headlong downward, towered up the sunny steep,
Then, with a sudden lift of the one great pinion,
Swung proudly to a curve, and from its height
Took half a mile of sunlight in one long sweep.

And we, so small on the swift immense hillside,
Stood tranced, until our souls arose uplifted
    On those far-sweeping, wide,
Strong curves of flight – swayed up and hugely drifted,
Were washed, made strong and beautiful in the tide
Of sun-bathed air. But far beneath, beholden
Through shining deeps of air, the fields were golden
And rosy burned the heather where cornfields ended.

And still those buzzards wheeled, while light withdrew
Out of the vales and to surging slopes ascended,
Till the loftiest flaming summit died to blue.

Hovering of Hawks

HENRY WILLIAMSON (1895–1977)

A cloud from the sea dragged over the mountain so that
the buzzards wheeling in the upper air were hidden,
and only their mewling cries came down. I suppose they
outsoared the cold autumnal vapours; they often sail in the
heavenly freeness a mile and more above the earth, broad
wings for ever lifted by the winds.

These big hawks are quite common in the West
Country; I have seen as many as ten pairs on the wing at
once. They are clumsy in the lower air, flapping heavily
and beating over the slopes of heather and gorse very much
like an owl. But when they attain to high solitude they
are transformed. Sometimes as they turn the sun throws a
golden lustre on their pinions.

All the British hawks that I have seen – kestrel,
sparrowhawk, merlin, peregrine falcon, buzzard, and
marsh harrier – hover to find their prey. Their hovering
may be prolonged, or for an instant only. The kestrel
leans on the wind, the sparrowhawk (I am referring to
those that hunt in the open) dashes down wind, swings
up, poises, then dashes down at his prey. The peregrine
falcon hangs high above the cliff slope or the inland fields.
He and his mate, hunting together, are like two black
anchor-heads. Even in a considerable wind they are not
disturbed. They remain fixed till something is seen, and
then they fall, head first, swifter and swifter, plunging at
an enormous rate. If they are within three hundred yards,
and the day is still, you may hear the hissing of the stoop.
They strike their victim and smash it, or miss altogether,

abandoning after three failed stoops. The male usually follows the female should she miss.

Buzzards – spanning nearly four feet – are the most graceful hoverers. They hang, with wings arched back, a few yards over the rabbit runs through the gorse and the bracken. A fairly steady breeze is needed to keep them stable. I have watched for more than a minute a buzzard hanging thus, moving only its tail. The secret of its poising is that it *falls* continually on the wind, pressing its breast into the flow to counteract the lifting impulse of its wings.

from *The Lone Swallows* (1922)

The Peregrine
J.A. BAKER (1926–1987)

Over orchards smelling of vinegary windfalls, busy with tits and bullfinches, a peregrine glides to perch in a river-bank alder. River shadows ripple on the spare, haunted face of the hawk in the water. They cross the cold eyes of the watching heron. Sunlight glints. The heron blinds the white river cornea with the spear of his bill. The hawk flies quickly upward to the breaking clouds.

Swerving and twisting away from the misty lower air, he rises to the first faint warmth of the sun, feels delicately for winghold on the sheer fall of sky. He is a tiercel, lean and long and supple-winged, the first of the year. He is the colour of yellow ochre sand and reddish-brown gravel. His big, brown, spaniel eyes shine wet in the sunlight, like circles of raw liver, embedded in the darker matt brown of the moustachial mask. He sweeps away to the west, following the gleaming curve of water. Laboriously I follow his trail of rising plover.

Swallows and martins call sharply, fly low; jays and magpies lurk and mutter in hedges; blackbirds splutter and scold. Where the valley widens, the flat fields are vibrant with tractors. Gulls and lapwings are following the plough. The sun shines from a clear sky flecked with high cirrus. The wind is moving round to the north. By the sudden calling of red-legged partridges and the clattering rise of woodpigeons, I know that the hawk is soaring and drifting southward along the woodland ridge. He is too high to be seen. I stay near the river, hoping he will come back into the wind. Crows in the elms are cursing and bobbing. Jackdaws cackle up from the hill, scatter, spiral away, till they are far out and small and silent in blue depths of sky. The hawk comes down to the river, a mile to the east; disappears into trees he left two hours before.

from *The Peregrine* (1967)

Hawk Roosting

TED HUGHES (1930–1998)

I sit in the top of the wood, my eyes closed.
Inaction, no falsifying dream
Between my hooked head and hooked feet:
Or in sleep rehearse perfect kills and eat.

The convenience of the high trees!
The air's buoyancy and the sun's ray
Are of advantage to me;
And the earth's face upward for my inspection.

My feet are locked upon the rough bark.
It took the whole of Creation
To produce my foot, my each feather:
Now I hold Creation in my foot

Or fly up, and revolve it all slowly –
I kill where I please because it is all mine.
There is no sophistry in my body:
My manners are tearing off heads –

The allotment of death.
For the one path of my flight is direct
Through the bones of the living.
No arguments assert my right:

The sun is behind me.
Nothing has changed since I began.
My eye has permitted no change.
I am going to keep things like this.

A Fleet of Eagles

CHRISTOPHER OKIGBO (1932–1967)

But the sunbird repeats
Over the oilbean shadows:

'A fleet of eagles
   over the oilbean shadows,
Holds the square
   under curse of their breath.

Beaks of bronze, wings
   of hard-tanned felt,
The eagles flow
   over man-mountains,
Steep walls of voices,
   horizons;
The eagles furrow
   dazzling over the voices
With wings like
   combs in the wind's hair

Out of the solitude, the fleet,
Out of the solitude,
Intangible like silk thread of sunlight,
The eagles ride low,
Resplendent … resplendent;
And small birds sing in shadows,
Wobbling under their bones…'

from 'Limits VIII' (1964)

Kes

Barry Hines (1939–2016)

Billy walked along the hedge bottom, searching for a way
through. He found a hole, and as he crawled through a
kestrel flew out of the monastery wall and veered away
across the fields behind the farm. Billy knelt and watched
it. In two blinks it was a speck in the distance; then it
wheeled and began to return. Billy hadn't moved a muscle
before it was slipping back across the face of the wall
towards the cart track.

Half-way across the orchard it started to glide upwards
in a shallow curve and alighted neatly on a telegraph pole
at the side of the cart track. It looked round, roused its
feathers, then crossed its wings over its back and settled.
Billy waited for it to turn away, then, watching it all
the time, he carefully stretched full length in the hedge
bottom. The hawk tensed and stood up straight, and stared
past the monastery into the distance. Billy looked in the
same direction. The sky was clear. A pair of magpies flew
up from the orchard and crossed to the wood, their quick
wing-beats seeming to just keep them airborne. They
took stance in a tree close by and started to chatter, each
sequence of chatterings sounding like one turn of a football
rattle. The hawk ignored them and continued to stare
into the distance. The sky was still clear. Then a speck
appeared on the horizon. It held like a star, then fell and
faded. Died. To reappear a moment later further along the
skyline. Fading and re-forming, sometimes no more than a
point in the texture of the sky. Billy squeezed his eyes and
rubbed them. On the telegraph pole the hawk was sleek

and still. The dot magnified slowly into its mate, circling and scanning the fields round the farm.

It braked and lay on the air looking down, primaries quivering to catch the currents, tail fanned, tilted towards the earth. Then, angling its wings, it slipped sideways a few yards, fluttered, and started to hover again. Persistently this time, hovering then dropping vertically in short bursts, until it closed its wings and stooped, a breath-taking stoop, down behind a wall. To rise again with its prey secure in its talons and head swiftly back across the fields. The falcon, alert on the pole, screamed and took off to meet it. They both screamed continuously as the distance closed between them, reaching a climax as they met and transferred the prey. The male disappeared over the wood. The falcon swooped high into a hole in the monastery wall. Billy noted the place carefully. A few seconds later the falcon reappeared and planed away over the fields, returning in a wide circle back to the telegraph pole.

… The hawk was waiting for him. As he unlocked the door she screamed and pressed her face to the bars. He selected the largest piece of beef, then, holding it firmly between finger and thumb with most of it concealed in his palm, he eased the door open and shoved his glove through the space. The hawk jumped on to his glove and attacked the meat. Billy swiftly followed his fist into the hut, secured the door behind him, and while the hawk was tearing at the fringe of beef, he attached her swivel and leash.

As soon as they got outside she looked up and tensed, feathers flat, eyes threatening. Billy stood still, whistling softly, waiting for her to relax and resume her feeding.

Then he walked round the back of the hut and held her high over his head as he climbed carefully over the fence. A tall hawthorn hedge bordered one side of the field, and the wind was strong and constant in the branches, but in the field it had been strained to a whisper. He reached the centre and unwound the leash from his glove, pulled it free of the swivel, then removed the swivel from the jesses and raised his fist. The hawk flapped her wings and fanned her tail, her claws still gripping the glove. Billy cast her off by nudging his glove upwards, and she banked away, completed a wide circuit then gained height rapidly, while he took the lure from his bag and unwound the line from the stick.

'Come on, Kes! Come on then!'

…Billy crouched down and made in towards the hawk along the lure line. He offered her a scrap of beef, and she stepped off the lure on to his glove. He allowed her to take the beef, then he stood up and cast her off again. She wheeled away, high round the field. Billy plucked the stick from the ground and began to swing the lure. The hawk turned and stooped at it. Billy watched her as she descended, waiting for the right moment as she accelerated rapidly towards him. Now. He straightened his arm and lengthened the line, throwing the lure into her path and sweeping it before her in a downward arc, then twitching it up too steep for her attack, making her throw up, her impetus carrying her high into the air. She turned and stooped again. Billy presented the lure again. And again. Each time smoothly before her, an inch before her so that the next wing-beat must catch it, or the next.

from *A Kestrel for a Knave* (1968)

To Become Invisible

Helen Macdonald (1970–)

Two wide, wild eyes stare at me for a fraction of a second,
and then they are gone. Before the hawk can work out
what the hell is happening she is trying to fly away as fast
as possible. Brought up short by her jesses she twitters
in high-pitched distress as the realisation of her hateful
circumstances strikes. She can't get away. I lift her back
onto the glove. Under her feathers is sinew, and bone, and
that fast-beating heart. She bates again. And again. I *hate*
this. In these first few minutes there's nothing you can do
but accept that you are terrifying the hawk when it is the
very opposite of everything you desire. After three more
bates my heart is beating like a fitting beast, but she's back
on the glove, beak open, eyes blazing. And then there is a
long moment of extraordinary intensity.

The goshawk is staring at me in mortal terror, and I can
feel the silences between both our heartbeats coincide. Her
eyes are luminous, silver in the gloom. Her beak is open.
She breathes hot hawk breath in my face. It smells of pepper
and musk and burned stone. Her feathers are half-raised
and her wings half-open, and her scaled yellow toes and
curved black talons grip the glove tightly. It feels like I'm
holding a flaming torch. I can feel the heat of her fear on
my face. She stares. She stares and stares. Seconds slow and
tick past. Her wings are dropped low; she crouches, ready
for flight. I don't look at her. I mustn't. What I am doing is
concentrating very hard on the process of *not being there*.

Here's one thing I know from years of training hawks:
one of the things you must learn to do is become invisible.

It's what you do when a fresh hawk sits on your left fist
with food beneath her feet, in a state of savage, defensive
fear. Hawks aren't social animals like dogs or horses; they
understand neither coercion nor punishment. The only way
to tame them is through positive reinforcement with gifts
of food. You want the hawk to eat the food you hold – it's
the first step in reclaiming her that will end with you
being hunting partners. But the space between the fear
and the food is a vast, vast gulf, and you have to cross it
together. ...

   To cross this space between fear and food, and to
somehow make possible an eventual concord between your
currently paralysed, immobile minds, you need – very
urgently – not to be there. You empty your mind and
become very still. You think of exactly nothing at all.
The hawk becomes a strange, hollow concept, as flat as a
snapshot or a schematic drawing, but at the same time,
as pertinent to your future as an angry high court judge.
Your gloved fist squeezes the meat a fraction, and you feel
the tiny imbalance of weight and you see out of the very
corner of your vision that she's looked down at it. And so,
remaining invisible, you make the food the only thing in
the room apart from the hawk; you're not there at all. And
what you hope is that she'll start eating, and you can very,
very slowly make yourself visible. Even if you don't move a
muscle, and just relax into a more normal frame of mind,
the hawk *knows*. It's extraordinary. It takes a long time to
be yourself, in the presence of a new hawk.

from H is for Hawk (2014)

A BIRDING YEAR
Autumn

from *Song Composed in August*

ROBERT BURNS (1759–1796)

Now westling winds, and slaught'ring guns
Bring Autumn's pleasant weather;
The moorcock springs on whirring wings
Among the blooming heather.
…
The partridge loves the fruitful fells,
The plover loves the mountains,
The woodcock haunts the lonely dells,
The soaring hern the fountains:
Thro' lofty groves the cushat roves,
The path of man to shun it;
The hazel bush o'erhangs the thrush,
The spreading thorn the linnet.

Thus ev'ry kind their pleasure find,
The savage and the tender;
Some social join, and leagues combine,
Some solitary wander:
Avaunt, away! the cruel sway,
Tyrannic man's dominion;
The sportsman's joy, the murd'ring cry,
The flutt'ring gory pinion!

Autumn Birds

JOHN CLARE (1793–1864)

The wild duck startles like a sudden thought,
And heron slow as if it might be caught.
The flopping crows on weary wings go by
And grey beard jackdaws noising as they fly.
The crowds of starnels whizz and hurry by,
And darken like a cloud the evening sky.
The larks like thunder rise and suthy round,
Then drop and nestle in the stubble ground.
The wild swan hurries hight and noises loud
With white neck peering to the evening clowd.
The weary rooks to distant woods are gone.
With lengths of tail the magpie winnows on
To neighbouring tree, and leaves the distant crow
While small birds nestle in the edge below.

When the Swallow Leaves

ROBERT CHAMBERS (1802–1871)

Nearly all our singing-birds have departed for sunnier lands
far over the sea, and the swallows are now preparing to
follow them, while, strange interchange, other birds visit
us which have been away all spring and summer. Some
days before the swallows leave us, they assemble together,
at certain places – generally beside a river – where they
wait fresh arrivals, until a flock of thousands is mustered;
and were not the same gathering going on at other places
beside, we might fancy that all the swallows that visit us
were assembled in one spot. One place they frequented,
which abounded in osier bolts, in our younger days, and
when up early angling, we have seen them rise in myriads
from the willows about six in the morning, and dividing
themselves into five or six companies, disperse in contrary
directions, when they remained away all day, beginning
to return about five, and continuing to come in until it
was nearly dark. No doubt this separation took place on
account of the scarcity of food, as sufficient could not be
found, without flying many miles from the riverside, where
they assembled. Every day the flock appeared to augment,
and we have no doubt that every division, on its return to
this great mustering ground, brought in many stragglers.

We have also often fancied that it was here the young
swallows exercised themselves, strengthening their wings
for the long journey that lay before them, by circling
flights and graceful evolutions, as if trying at times which
could come nearest the water at the greatest speed without
touching a drop with either breast or pinions. We also

came to the conclusion that all the young ones did not accompany the divisions that went away every day in search of food, but only a portion – as thousands retrained – and that those which went out one day rested the next, and had their turn on the second morning, or each alternate day. They seldom remained later than the middle of October, and when they left for good, went away all together, in the direction of the south. A few generally remained for a day or two, then went off in the same direction. Dead swallows were generally picked up among the willows after the flock had migrated.

Earliest amongst the fresh arrivals is the woodcock, who generally reaches the end of his journey in the night, and very weary and jaded he appears. Seldom is he ever seen to land, though he has been found hiding himself near the coast, in so exhausted a state as to be run down, and taken by hand. But he does not remain by the sea-side a day longer than he is compelled, where, having recruited himself a little, he sets off to visit his former haunts. The snipe also arrives about the same time, and is found in the haunts of the woodcock, on high moors and hills, while the season is mild, and in low, warm, sheltered localities when the weather is severe.

In October the redwing reaches us, and if the autumn is fine and warm, its song may often be heard. Its favourite haunts are parks, and secure places, abounding in clumps of trees, where it feeds on worms, and such like soft food, so long as it can be found; never feeding on berries unless they are forced by the frost, then they soon perish. The early arrival of the fieldfare is considered by country people a sure sign of a hard winter, especially if there is a large crop of heps and haws, which they say, reverentially, Providence has stored up for them beforehand. We think it is a surer sign, that, in the country they have quitted, severe weather has set in earlier than usual.

from *The Book of Days* (1802–07)

To-day the Lark Sings Again

Henry David Thoreau (1817–1862)

Sept. 29, 1842. To-day the lark sings again down in the meadow, and the robin peeps, and the bluebirds, old and young, have revisited their box, as if they would fain repeat the summer without the intervention of winter, if Nature would let them.

Oct. 7, 1842. A little girl has just brought me a purple finch or American linnet. These birds are now moving south. It reminds me of the pine and spruce, and the juniper and cedar on whose berries it feeds. It has the crimson hues of the October evenings, and its plumage still shines as if it had caught and preserved some of their tints (beams?). We know it chiefly as a traveller. It reminds me of many things I had forgotten. Many a serene evening lies snugly packed under its wing.

The Birds are Consulting about
their Migrations

GEORGE ELIOT (1819–1880)

Letter to Miss Lewis, 1st Oct. 1841

Is not this a true autumn day? Just the still melancholy that
I love – that makes life and nature harmonize. The birds
are consulting about their migrations, the trees are putting
on the hectic or the pallid hues of decay, and begin to
strew the ground, that one's very footsteps may not disturb
the repose of earth and air, while they give us a scent
that is a perfect anodyne to the restless spirit. Delicious
autumn! My very soul is wedded to it, and if I were a bird
I would fly about the earth seeking the successive autumns.

The Birds of San Michele

AXEL MUNTHE (1857–1949)

They came just before sunrise. All they asked for was to
rest for a while after their long flight across the Mediterranean, the goal of the journey was so far away, the land
where they were born and where they were to raise their
young. They came in thousands: woodpigeons, thrushes,
turtle-doves, waders, quails, golden orioles, skylarks,
nightingales, wagtails, chaffinches, swallows, warblers,
redbreasts and many other tiny artists on their way to give
spring concerts to the silent forests and fields in the north.
A couple of hours later they fluttered helplessly in the nets
the cunning of man had stretched all over the island from
the cliffs by the sea high up to the slopes of Monte Solaro

and Monte Barbarossa. ... The mountain of Barbarossa is now a bird sanctuary. Thousands of tired birds of passage are resting on its slopes every spring and autumn, safe from man and beast. The dogs of San Michele are forbidden to bark while the birds are resting on the mountain. The cats are never let out of the kitchen except with a little alarm-bell tied round their necks.

from *The Story of San Michele* (1929)

The Call of the South
KENNETH GRAHAME (1859–1932)

In the osiers which fringed the bank he spied a swallow sitting. Presently it was joined by another, and then by a third; and the birds, fidgeting restlessly on their bough, talked together earnestly and low.

'What, *already*?' said the Rat, strolling up to them. 'What's the hurry? I call it simply ridiculous.'

'O, we're not off yet, if that's what you mean,' replied the first swallow. 'We're only making plans and arranging things. Talking it over, you know – what route we're taking this year, and where we'll stop, and so on. That's half the fun!'

'Fun?' said the Rat; 'now that's just what I don't understand. If you've *got* to leave this pleasant place, and your friends who will miss you, and your snug homes that you've just settled into, why, when the hour strikes I've no doubt you'll go bravely, and face all the trouble and discomfort and change and newness, and make believe that you're not very unhappy. But to want to talk about it, or even think about it, till you really need –'

'No, you don't understand, naturally,' said the second swallow. 'First, we feel it stirring within us, a sweet unrest; then back come the recollections one by one, like homing pigeons. They flutter through our dreams at night, they fly with us in our wheelings and circlings by day. We hunger to inquire of each other, to compare notes and assure ourselves that it was all really true, as one by one the scents and sounds and names of long-forgotten places come gradually back and beckon to us.'

'Couldn't you stop on for just this year?' suggested the Water Rat, wistfully. 'We'll all do our best to make you feel at home. You've no idea what good times we have here, while you are far away.'

'I tried "stopping on" one year,' said the third swallow. 'I had grown so fond of the place that when the time came I hung back and let the others go on without me. For a few weeks it was all well enough, but afterwards, O the weary length of the nights! The shivering, sunless days! The air so clammy and chill, and not an insect in an acre of it! No, it was no good; my courage broke down, and one cold, stormy night I took wing, flying well inland on account of the strong easterly gales. It was snowing hard as I beat through the passes of the great mountains, and I had a stiff fight to win through; but never shall I forget the blissful feeling of the hot sun again on my back as I sped down to the lakes that lay so blue and placid below me, and the taste of my first fat insect! The past was like a bad dream; the future was all happy holiday as I moved Southwards week by week, easily, lazily, lingering as long as I dared, but always heeding the call! No, I had had my warning; never again did I think of disobedience.'

'Ah, yes, the call of the South, of the South!' twittered
the other two dreamily. 'Its songs, its hues, its radiant air!'

from *The Wind in the Willows* (1908)

A Pair of Swallows, My Only Visitors

EDITH WHARTON (1862–1937)

Whoever would understand Marrakech must begin by
mounting at sunset to the roof of the Bahia.

Outspread below lies the oasis-city of the south, flat
and vast as the great nomad camp it really is, its low roofs
extending on all sides to a belt of blue palms ringed with
desert. …

The beauty of Moroccan palaces is made up of details
of ornament and refinements of sensuous delight too
numerous to record; but to get an idea of their general
character it is worthwhile to cross the Court of Cypresses
at the Bahia and follow a series of low-studded passages
that turn on themselves till they reach the centre of
the labyrinth. Here, passing by a low padlocked door
leading to a crypt, and known as the 'Door of the Vizier's
Treasure-House', one comes on a painted portal that opens
into a still more secret sanctuary: The apartment of the
Grand Vizier's Favourite.

This lovely prison, from which all sight and sound of
the outer world are excluded, is built about an atrium
paved with disks of turquoise and black and white. Water
trickles from a central *vasca* of alabaster into a hexagonal
mosaic channel in the pavement. The walls, which are at
least twenty-five feet high, are roofed with painted beams

resting on panels of traceried stucco in which is set a clerestory of jewelled glass. On each side of the atrium are long recessed rooms closed by vermilion doors painted with gold arabesques and vases of spring flowers; and into these shadowy inner rooms, spread with rugs and divans and soft pillows, no light comes except when their doors are opened into the atrium. In this fabulous place it was my good luck to be lodged while I was at Marrakech.

In a climate where, after the winter snow has melted from the Atlas, every breath of air for long months is a flame of fire, these enclosed rooms in the middle of the palaces are the only places of refuge from the heat. Even in October the temperature of the favourite's apartment was deliciously reviving after a morning in the bazaars or the dusty streets, and I never came back to its wet tiles and perpetual twilight without the sense of plunging into a deep sea-pool.

From far off, through circuitous corridors, came the scent of citron-blossom and jasmine, with sometimes a bird's song before dawn, sometimes a flute's wail at sunset, and always the call of the muezzin in the night; but no sunlight reached the apartment except in remote rays through the clerestory, and no air except through one or two broken panes.

Sometimes, lying on my divan, and looking out through the vermilion doors, I used to surprise a pair of swallows dropping down from their nest in the cedar-beams to preen themselves on the fountain's edge or in the channels of the pavement; for the roof was full of birds who came and went through the broken panes of the clerestory. Usually they were my only visitors.

from *In Morocco* (1920)

The Evening Flight of Starlings

EDWARD GREY, *Viscount of Fallodon* (1862–1933)

The evening flight of starlings over their chosen roosting-place in autumn and winter is one of the marvels of flying. The birds assemble, small parties coming to the chosen spot from any direction after the business of the day is over. They then fly at speed above the roosting-place: a vast globe, it may be, of some thousands of birds. They fly close together, and there are many evolutions and swift turns, yet there is no collision: the impulse to each quick movement or change of direction seems to seize every bird simultaneously. It is as if for the time being each bird had ceased to be a separate entity and had become a part of one sentient whole: one great body, the movement of whose parts was co-ordinated by one impulse or one will affecting them all at the same moment. For some time this wonderful performance continues, then as the globe passes over the laurels a little avalanche of starlings descends, making a rushing noise as it penetrates the stiff leaves. Party after party of starlings now detaches itself and descends each time that the globe passes over the spot, till at length there is but one small party left flying, and this, too, presently descends. There are now hundreds, or it may be thousands, of birds in the evergreens, and for a while there is fuss and chatter; so loud is the noise that I have known it mistaken at a little distance for the sound of a waterfall. I have spoken of laurels, because it is these that the starlings choose at Fallodon, but they may select any thicket of evergreens. … It is not apparent that this evening flight of starlings serves any purpose except that of pleasure, but it occurs in late autumn and winter, and cannot therefore be quite analogous to the joy flights of spring and the pairing season.

from The Charm of Birds (1927)

The Wild Swans at Coole

WILLIAM BUTLER YEATS (1865–1939)

The trees are in their autumn beauty,
The woodland paths are dry,
Under the October twilight the water
Mirrors a still sky;
Upon the brimming water among the stones
Are nine-and-fifty swans.

The nineteenth Autumn has come upon me
Since I first made my count;
I saw, before I had well finished,
All suddenly mount
And scatter wheeling in great broken rings
Upon their clamorous wings.

I have looked upon those brilliant creatures,
And now my heart is sore.
All's changed since I, hearing at twilight,
The first time on this shore,
The bell-beat of their wings above my head,
Trod with a lighter tread.

Unwearied still, lover by lover,
They paddle in the cold,
Companionable streams or climb the air;
Their hearts have not grown old;
Passion or conquest, wander where they will,
Attend upon them still.

But now they drift on the still water,
Mysterious, beautiful;
Among what rushes will they build,
By what lake's edge or pool
Delight men's eyes when I awake some day
To find they have flown away?

Up-hill Planters in the Sierra Nevada

Joseph Grinnell (1877–1939)

The next two days, October 12 and 13, my companion,
Dr. Eric Hill, and I spent seeking pocket-gophers down
near Three Rivers, about 1,000 feet altitude, in the valley
of the lower Kaweah River. Here another kind of oak, the
blue oak, abounded, and we observed that there was a fairly
good crop of its acorns, though not borne as uniformly as
those of the black oak in the life-zone above. Very many
of the blue oaks had produced no acorns that season.
Especially was this true of the trees far up the hillsides
above the valley bottom. Some of the trees had produced a
few acorns. Those trees which were bearing most heavily
were those of larger, thriftier-looking condition, down
toward the river bottom. Of certain possible bearing on
our problem, this season was a dry one; and furthermore it
was the latest of a series of dry years.

As we tended our trap-lines, run in all the different
types of soil within reach, we became aware of the
presence and especially the activities of California Jays
(*Aphelocoma californica*). These activities looked into, became
of deep significance to us; for here, indeed, was the agency
at this particular place, at this particular time, of transpor-
tation of acorns up-hill. The jays we saw to be centering
their interest in those most abundantly fruiting trees
down in the bottom of the canyon. There the birds were
gathering the acorns and carrying them up the slopes, to
be ensconced in various hidey-holes, some of them to be
buried, after the well-known blue-jay tradition, in the
ground of open spaces on the hillsides. From morning to

evening, individual birds were almost constantly in sight when we looked out of the auto cabin where we worked, 150 yards from the river.

Every bird going up-slope bore an acorn lengthwise in its bill; every bird in return course was empty-billed. If I had only thought of it, here was a chance for counting birds, and their loads, in sight, during, say, a three-hour period; and then computing the bushels of blue-oak acorns being elevated by the jays perhaps hundreds of feet each October day in that one valley.

from 'Up-hill Planters', *Condor* (1936)

Autumn Woods

EDWARD THOMAS (1878–1917)

Beneath the rosy-clouded sky come black battalions of rooks, with their attendant daws, almost equally numerous. Night after night, with striking regularity, vast numbers of these broad-winged birds pursue their way to the elms and beeches that form their rendezvous.

When their hereditary roost-trees are reached they mount aloft and, with an eccentric turn, swoop towards the beech-tops, apparently to plunge amongst them, but, turning abruptly, they rise again, to repeat their diving movements. In these manoeuvres, oft-repeated, jackdaws accompany the rooks, performing strange aerial feats. Sometimes they race and plunge like nesting peewits. For an hour at a stretch rooks and daws execute these strange evolutions, and the former lose for the time all their usual unwieldiness.

As the daylight continues to fade the birds still keep high in air, while some few descend to the sward, which they dot in the distance with doubtful specks of black. When at last the faint gleam of sunset disappears from the woods, the clangorous rooks in the swaying trees are beating assembly for the night.

from The Woodland Life (1897)

The Wild Ducks Migrate

Antoine de Saint-Exupéry (1900–1944)

When the wild ducks or the wild geese migrate in their season, a strange tide rises in the territories over which they sweep. As if magnetized by the great triangular flight, the barnyard fowl leap a foot or two into the air and try to fly. The call of the wild strikes them with the force of a harpoon and a vestige of savagery quickens their blood. All the ducks on the farm are transformed for an instant into migrant birds, and into those hard little heads, till now filled with humble images of pools and worms and barnyards, there swims a sense of continental expanse, of the breadth of seas and the salt taste of the ocean wind. The duck totters to right and left in its wire enclosure, gripped by a sudden passion to perform the impossible and a sudden love whose object is a mystery.

from Wind, Sand and Stars (1939)

The Storks' Migration

EDWARD PLATT (1968–)

As I gazed at the crest of the hill to our right, a blizzard of
dark dots appeared from behind it and swept towards us,
moulding themselves to the slope stretching out into the
plain. I checked my watch – it was ten past three – and
when I looked up again, it took me a moment to relocate
the birds. Already, they were in the middle of the valley,
streaming out behind one another in a fluid formation, like a
flattened speech balloon.

It was astonishing to think how far – and how fast – they
had travelled. They had left southern Africa while I was
still in England and, flying for an average of nine hours a
day, at forty kilometres per hour, they had pushed through
eastern Africa to their pre-wintering grounds in Sudan and
Chad. From there, they turned north-west towards Egypt,
following the Nile from Aswan to Qina, before crossing
the Sinai peninsula and entering southern Israel. Only this
morning, they had been in the vast expanse of the Negev
Desert and now they were passing our station on the slopes
of Mount Gilboa.

… By tomorrow, they would be over Lebanon and Syria,
where they would turn north-west, cutting the corner of
the Mediterranean and flying above the Turkish port of
Iskenderum. They would cross the Bosporus at Istanbul, or
the west side of the Sea of Marmara, and in Bulgaria, they
would reach a turning point: some flocks would keep going
into Central and Southern Europe and others would turn
east, towards nesting grounds in western Russia.

from 'The Migration' (2008)

BIRDS & US

Corinna's Pet Parrot

OVID (43 BCE–17 CE)

The parrot, the imitative bird sent from the Indians of the East, is dead; come in flocks to his obsequies, ye birds. Come, affectionate denizens of air, and beat your breasts with your wings; and with your hard claws disfigure your delicate features. Let your rough feathers be torn in place of your sorrowing hair; instead of the long trumpet, let your songs resound.

Why, Philomela, are you complaining of the cruelty of *Tereus*, the Ismarian tyrant? *Surely*, that grievance is worn out by its *length of* years. Turn your attention to the sad end of a bird so prized. It is a great cause of sorrow, but, *still*, that so old. All, who poise yourselves in your career in the liquid air; but you, above the rest, affectionate turtle-dove, lament him. Throughout life there was a firm attachment between you, and your prolonged and lasting friendship endured to the end. What the Phoecian youth was to the Argive Orestes, the same, parrot, was the turtle-dove to you, so long as it was allowed *by fate*.

But what *matters* that friendship? What the beauty of your rare plumage? What your voice so ingenious at imitating sounds? What avails it that *ever* since you were given, you pleased my mistress? Unfortunate pride of *all* birds, you are indeed laid low. With your feathers you could outvie the green emerald, having your purple beak tinted with the ruddy saffron. There was no bird on earth more skilled at imitating sounds; so prettily did you utter words with your lisping notes. …

Why should I mention the affectionate prayers of my anxious mistress in your behalf; prayers borne over the seas by the stormy North wind? The seventh day was come, that was doomed to give no morrow; and now stood your Destiny, with her distaff all uncovered. And yet your words did not die away, in your faltering mouth; as you died, your tongue cried aloud, 'Corinna, farewell!'

from *Amores*, trans. Henry T. Riley

So many and so useful and pleasant to mankind

IZAAK WALTON (1593–1683)

[T]he very birds of the air, those that be not Hawks, are both so many and so useful and pleasant to mankind, that I must not let them pass without some observations. ...

As first the Lark, when she means to rejoice, to cheer herself and those that hear her; she then quits the earth, and sings as she ascends higher into the air and having ended her heavenly employment, grows then mute, and sad, to think she must descend to the dull earth, which she would not touch, but for necessity.

How do the Blackbird and Thrassel with their melodious voices bid welcome to the cheerful Spring, and in their fixed months warble forth such ditties as no art or instrument can reach to!

Nay, the smaller birds also do the like in their particular seasons, as namely the Laverock, the Tit-lark, the little Linnet, and the honest Robin that loves mankind both alive and dead.

But the Nightingale, another of my airy creatures, breathes such sweet loud musick out of her little instrumental throat, that it might make mankind to think miracles are not ceased. He that at midnight, when the very labourer sleeps securely, should hear, as I have very often, the clear airs, the sweet descants, the natural rising and falling, the doubling and redoubling of her voice, might well be lifted above earth, and say, 'Lord, what musick hast thou provided for the Saints in Heaven, when thou affordest bad men such musick on Earth!'

from *The Compleat Angler* (1653)

from *Auguries of Innocence*

WILLIAM BLAKE (1757–1827)

A Robin Red breast in a Cage
Puts all Heaven in a Rage.
A Dove house filld with Doves & Pigeons
Shudders Hell thro all its regions.
…
A Skylark wounded in the wing
A Cherubim does cease to sing.
The Game Cock clipt & armed for fight
Does the Rising Sun affright.
…
The Owl that calls upon the Night
Speaks the Unbeliever's fright.
He who shall hurt the little Wren
Shall never be belovd by Men.

Watching the Bittern

ROBERT MUDIE (1777–1842)

On a fine clear day in the early part of the season, when the winds of March have dried the heath … it is not unpleasant to ramble towards the abode of the bittern… The reeds begin to rustle with the little winds, in which the day settles account with the night; but there is a shorter and a sharper rustle, accompanied by the brush of rather a powerful wing. You look round the dim horizon, but there is no bird: another rustle of the wing, and another, still weaker and weaker, but not a moving thing between you and the sky around. You feel rather disappointed – foolish, if you are daring; fearful if you are timid. Anon, a burst of uncouth and savage laughter breaks over you, piercingly, or rather gratingly loud, and so unwonted and odd, that it sounds as if the voices of a bull and a horse were combined, the former breaking down his bellow to suit the neigh of the latter, in mocking you from the sky.

That is the love-song of the bittern, with which he serenades his mate; and uncouth and harsh as it sounds to you, that mate hears it with far more pleasure than she would the sweetest chorus of the grove; and when the surprise with which you are at first taken is over, you begin to discover that there is a sort of modulation in the singular sound. As the bird utters it he wheels in a spiral, expanding his voice as the loops widen, and sinking it as they close; and though you can just dimly discover him between you and the zenith, it is worth while to lie down on your back, and watch the style of his flight, which is as fine as it is peculiar.

from *The Feathered Tribes of the British Isles* (1841)

Fishing Cormorants in China

ROBERT FORTUNE (1813–1880)

There were two small boats, containing one man and
about ten or twelve birds in each. The birds were standing
perched on the sides of the little boat, and apparently
had just arrived at the fishing ground, and were about to
commence operations. They were now ordered out of the
boats by their masters; and so well trained were they, that
they went on the water immediately, scattered themselves
over the canal, and began to look for fish. They have a
beautiful sea-green eye, and, quick as lightning, they see
and dive upon the finny tribe, which, once caught in the
sharp-notched bill of the bird, never by any possibility can
escape. The cormorant now rises to the surface with the
fish in its bill, and the moment he is seen by the Chinaman
he is called back to the boat. As docile as a dog, he swims
after his master, and allows himself to be pulled into the
San-pan, where he disgorges his prey, and again resumes
his labours. And, what is more wonderful still, if one of
the cormorants gets hold of a fish of large size, so large
that he would have some difficulty in taking it to the boat,
some of the others, seeing his dilemma, hasten to his
assistance, and with their efforts united capture the animal
and haul him off to the boat. Sometimes a bird seemed to
get lazy or playful, and swam about without attending to
his business; and then the Chinaman, with a long bamboo,
which he also used for propelling the boat, struck the
water near where the bird was, without, however, hurting
him, calling out to him at the same time in an angry tone.
Immediately, like the truant school-boy who neglects his

lessons and is found out, the cormorant gives up his play and resumes his labours.

from Three Years' Wanderings in the Northern Provinces of China (1847)

An Unrequited Attachment

GEORGE ELIOT (1819–1880)

Letter to Miss Sara Hennell, 20th Feb. 1861

My only pleasure away from our own hearth is going to the Zoological Gardens. Mr Lewes is a fellow, so we turn in there several times a week; and I find the birds and beasts there most congenial to my spirit. There is a Shoebill, a great bird of grotesque ugliness, whose topknot looks brushed up to a point with an exemplary deference to the demands of society, but who, I am sure, has no idea that he looks the handsomer for it. I cherish an unrequited attachment to him.

Miss Nightingale's Owl

MOUNTSTUART GRANT DUFF (1829–1906)

1862

Lady Verney is Miss Nightingale's sister, and one of the curiosities of the house is a manuscript by Lady Verney describing the life and adventures of her sister's owl Athena, which, bought for 6 lepta from some children into whose hands it had dropped out of its nest in the Parthenon, was brought by Miss Nightingale to Trieste, with a slip of a plane from the Ilissus, and a cicala. At Vienna the owl ate the cicala and was mesmerised, much to the improvement of its temper. At Prague a waiter was heard to say that 'this is the bird which all English ladies carry with them, because it tells them when they are to die.' It came to England by Berlin, lived at Embley, Lea Hurst, and in London, travelled in Germany, and stayed at Carlsbad while its mistress was at Kaiserswerth. It died the very day she was to have started for Scutari (her departure was delayed two days), 'and the only tear that she shed during that tremendous week was when they put the little body into her hand.' 'Poor little beastie,' she said, 'it was odd how much I loved you.'

from *Notes from a Diary, 1851–1872* (1897)

Hope is the thing with feathers

EMILY DICKINSON (1830–1886)

Hope is the thing with feathers
That perches in the soul,
And sings the tune without the words,
And never stops at all,

And sweetest in the gale is heard;
And sore must be the storm
That could abash the little bird
That kept so many warm.

I've heard it in the chillest land,
And on the strangest sea;
Yet, never, in extremity,
It asked a crumb of me.

Mrs d'Urberville's Birds

Thomas Hardy (1840–1928)

'Mrs d'Urberville wants the fowls as usual,' she said; but perceiving that Tess did not quite understand, she explained, 'Mis'ess is a old lady, and blind.'

'Blind!' said Tess.

Almost before her misgiving at the news could find time to shape itself she took, under her companion's direction, two of the most beautiful of the Hamburghs in her arms, and followed the maid-servant, who had likewise taken two, to the adjacent mansion, which, though ornate and imposing, showed traces everywhere on this side that some occupant of its chambers could bend to the love of dumb creatures – feathers floating within view of the front, and hen-coops standing on the grass.

In a sitting-room on the ground-floor, ensconced in an armchair with her back to the light, was the owner and mistress of the estate, a white-haired woman of not more than sixty, or even less, wearing a large cap. She had the mobile face frequent in those whose sight has decayed by stages, has been laboriously striven after, and reluctantly let go, rather than the stagnant mien apparent in persons long sightless or born blind. Tess walked up to this lady with her feathered charges – one sitting on each arm.

'Ah, you are the young woman come to look after my birds?' said Mrs d'Urberville, recognizing a new footstep. 'I hope you will be kind to them. My bailiff tells me you are quite the proper person. Well, where are they? Ah, this is Strut! But he is hardly so lively today, is he? He is alarmed at being handled by a stranger, I suppose. And

Phena too – yes, they are a little frightened – aren't you, dears? But they will soon get used to you.'

While the old lady had been speaking Tess and the other maid, in obedience to her gestures, had placed the fowls severally in her lap, and she had felt them over from head to tail, examining their beaks, their combs, the manes of the cocks, their wings, and their laws. Her touch enabled her to recognize them in a moment, and to discover if a single feather were crippled or draggled. She handled their crops, and knew what they had eaten, and if too little or too much; her face enacting a vivid pantomime of the criticisms passing in her mind.

The birds that the two girls had brought in were duly returned to the yard, and the process was repeated till all the pet cocks and hens had been submitted to the old woman – Hamburghs, Bantams, Cochins, Brahmas, Dorkings, and such other sorts as were in fashion just then – her perception of each visitor being seldom at fault as she received the bird upon her knees.

from *Tess of the d'Urbervilles* (1891)

'*Ho–ke-kyo!*'

LAFCADIO HEARN (1850–1904)

'*Ho–ke-kyo!*'

My uguisu is awake at last, and utters his morning prayer. You do not know what an uguisu is? An uguisu is a holy little bird that professes Buddhism. All uguisu have professed Buddhism from time immemorial; all uguisu preach alike to men the excellence of the divine Sutra.

'*Ho—ke-kyo!*'

In the Japanese tongue, *Ho—ke-kyo*; in Sanscrit, Saddharma Pundarika: 'The Sutra of the Lotus of the Good Law', the divine book of the Nichiren sect. Very brief, indeed, is my little feathered Buddhist's confession of faith – only the sacred name reiterated over and over again like a litany, with liquid bursts of twittering between.

'*Ho—ke-kyo!*'

Only this one phrase, but how deliciously he utters it! With what slow amorous ecstasy he dwells upon its golden syllables! It hath been written: 'He who shall keep, read, teach, or write this Sutra shall obtain eight hundred good qualities of the Eye. He shall see the whole Triple Universe down to the great hell Aviki, and up to the extremity of existence. He shall obtain twelve hundred good qualities of the Ear. He shall hear all sounds in the Triple Universe, – sounds of gods, goblins, demons, and beings not human.'

'*Ho—ke-kyo!*'

A single word only. But it is also written: 'He who shall joyfully accept but a single word from this Sutra, incalculably greater shall be his merit than the merit of one who should supply all beings in the four hundred thousand Asankhyeyas of worlds with all the necessaries for happiness.'

'*Ho—ke-kyo!*'

Always he makes a reverent little pause after uttering it and before shrilling out his ecstatic warble – his bird-hymn of praise. First the warble; then a pause of about five seconds; then a slow, sweet, solemn utterance of the holy name in a tone as of meditative wonder; then another pause; then another wild, rich, passionate warble.

Could you see him, you would marvel how so powerful
and penetrating a soprano could ripple from so minute
a throat; for he is one of the very tiniest of all feathered
singers, yet his chant can be heard far across the broad
river, and children going to school pause daily on the
bridge, a whole cho away, to listen to his song.

from *Glimpses of an Unfamiliar Japan* (1894)

from *The Bird Market*

ANTON CHEKHOV (1860–1904)

There is a small square near the monastery of the Holy
Birth which is called Trubnoy, or simply Truboy; there
is a market there on Sundays. Hundreds of sheepskins,
wadded coats, fur caps, and chimneypot hats swarm there,
like crabs in a sieve. There is the sound of the twitter of
birds in all sorts of keys, recalling the spring. If the sun
is shining, and there are no clouds in the sky, the singing
of the birds and the smell of hay make a more vivid
impression, and this reminder of spring sets one thinking
and carries one's fancy far, far away. Along one side of
the square there stands a string of waggons. The waggons
are loaded, not with hay, not with cabbages, nor with
beans, but with goldfinches, siskins, larks, blackbirds and
thrushes, bluetits, bullfinches. All of them are hopping
about in rough, home-made cages, twittering and looking
with envy at the free sparrows. The goldfinches cost five
kopecks, the siskins are rather more expensive, while the
value of the other birds is quite indeterminate.

'How much is a lark?'

The seller himself does not know the value of a lark. He scratches his head and asks whatever comes into it, a rouble, or three kopecks, according to the purchaser. There are expensive birds too. A faded old blackbird, with most of its feathers plucked out of its tail, sits on a dirty perch. He is dignified, grave, and motionless as a retired general. He has waved his claw in resignation to his captivity long ago, and looks at the blue sky with indifference. Probably, owing to this indifference, he is considered a sagacious bird. He is not to be bought for less than forty kopecks. Schoolboys, workmen, young men in stylish greatcoats, and bird-fanciers in incredibly shabby caps, in ragged trousers that are turned up at the ankles, and look as though they had been gnawed by mice, crowd round the birds, splashing through the mud. The young people and the workmen are sold hens for cocks, young birds for old ones. ... They know very little about birds. But there is no deceiving the bird-fancier. He sees and understands his bird from a distance.

'There is no relying on that bird,' a fancier will say, looking into a siskin's beak, and counting the feathers on its tail. 'He sings now, it's true, but what of that? I sing in company too. No, my boy, shout, sing to me without company; sing in solitude, if you can. ... You give me that one yonder that sits and holds its tongue! Give me the quiet one! That one says nothing, so he thinks the more. ...'

trans. Constance Garnett (1922)

Birdlife at Tinki-Dzong

CHARLES KENNETH HOWARD-BURY (1881–1963),
GEORGE H. LEIGH-MALLORY (1886–1924)
& A.F.R. WOLLASTON (1875–1930)

The bar-headed geese and the wild duck here were
extraordinarily tame, allowing us to approach within five
yards of them and showing no signs of fear. They would
come and waddle round our tents, picking up any scraps of
food. …

Tinki-Dzong is a veritable bird sanctuary. The Dzong
itself is a rambling fort covering a dozen or so of acres,
and about its walls nest hundreds of birds – ravens,
magpies, red-billed choughs, tree-sparrows, hoopoes,
Indian redstarts, Hodgson's pied wagtails and rock-doves.
In the shallow pool outside the Dzong were swimming
bar-headed geese and ruddy shelducks, with families of
young birds, all as tame as domestic poultry. A pair of
white storks was seen here in June, but they did not appear
to be breeding. In the autumn the lakes in this neighbourhood are the resort of large packs of wigeon, gadwall
and pochard. The Jongpen explained to us that it was the
particular wish of the Dalai Lama that no birds should be
molested here, and for several years two lamas lived at
Tinki, whose special business it was to protect the birds.

from *Mount Everest, the Reconnaissance, 1921* (1922)

Wart and the Owl

T.H. WHITE (1906–1964)

Merlyn took off his pointed hat when he came into this chamber, because it was too high for the roof, and immediately there was a scamper in one of the dark corners and a flap of soft wings, and a tawny owl was sitting on the black skull-cap which protected the top of his head.

'Oh, what a lovely owl!' cried the Wart.

But when he went up to it and held out his hand, the owl grew half as tall again, stood up as stiff as a poker, closed its eyes so that there was only the smallest slit to peep through – as you are in the habit of doing when told to shut your eyes at hide-and-seek – and said in a doubtful voice:

'There is no owl.'

Then it shut its eyes entirely and looked the other way.

'It is only a boy,' said Merlyn.

'There is no boy,' said the owl hopefully, without turning round.

The Wart was so startled by finding that the owl could talk that he forgot his manners and came closer still. At this the bird became so nervous that it made a mess on Merlyn's head – the whole room was quite white with droppings – and flew off to perch on the farthest tip of the corkindrill's tail, out of reach.

'We see so little company,' explained the magician, wiping his head with half a worn-out pair of pyjamas which he kept for that purpose, 'that Archimedes is a little shy of strangers. Come, Archimedes, I want you to meet a friend of mine called Wart.'

Here he held out his hand to the owl, who came waddling like a goose along the corkindrill's back – he waddled with this rolling gait so as to keep his tail from being damaged – and hopped down to Merlyn's finger with every sign of reluctance.

'Hold out your finger and put it behind his legs. No, lift it up under his train.'

When the Wart had done this, Merlyn moved the owl gently backward, so that the boy's finger pressed against its legs from behind, and it either had to step back on the finger or get pushed off its balance altogether. It stepped back. The Wart stood there delighted, while the furry feet held tight on his finger and the sharp claws prickled his skin.

'Say how d'you do properly,' said Merlyn.

'I will not,' said Archimedes, looking the other way and holding tight.

'Oh, he *is* lovely,' said the Wart again. 'Have you had him long?'

'Archimedes has stayed with me since he was small, indeed since he had a tiny head like a chicken's.'

'I wish he would talk to me.'

'Perhaps if you were to give him this mouse here, politely, he might learn to know you better.'

Merlyn took a dead mouse out of his skull-cap – 'I always keep them there, and worms too, for fishing. I find it most convenient' – and handed it to the Wart, who held it out rather gingerly toward Archimedes. The nutty curved beak looked as if it were capable of doing damage, but Archimedes looked closely at the mouse, blinked at the Wart, moved nearer on the finger, closed his eyes and leaned forward. He stood there with closed eyes and an expression of rapture on his face, as if he were saying Grace, and then, with the absurdest sideways nibble, took the morsel so gently that he would not have broken a soap bubble. He remained leaning forward with closed eyes, with the mouse suspended from his beak, as if he were not sure what to do with it. Then he lifted his right foot – he was right-handed, though people say only men are – and took hold of the mouse. He held it up like a boy holding a stick of rock or a constable with his truncheon, looked at it, nibbled its tail. He turned it round so that it was head first, for the Wart had offered it the wrong way round, and gave one gulp. He looked round at the company with the tail hanging out of the corner of his mouth – as much as to say, 'I wish you would not all stare at me so' – turned his head away, politely swallowed the tail, scratched his sailor's beard with his left toe, and began to ruffle out his feathers.

'Let him alone,' said Merlyn. 'Perhaps he does not want to be friends with you until he knows what you are like. With owls, it is never easy-come and easy-go.'

from *The Once and Future King* (1958)

The Biography of a Runner Duck
MURIEL KENNY (*20th century*)

Humphry, an Indian runner duck, was given to us when six weeks old, and proved through three years as intelligent, affectionate, and companionable a pet as we have ever known. He had no bird-companions and quickly developed a passion for human society. He would escort one round the garden in embarrassingly close attendance, maintaining a low conversational twitter of unutterable content. His mistress alone he distinguished by holding her skirt in his beak as he walked beside her, and on her return from a holiday he would greet her with extravagant manifestations of delight, jumping around her, rubbing his head against her, and making little snatches at her dress. He had a special salutation for well-known friends, a sudden profound curtsey accompanied by loud quacking and raising of the crest feathers. He and the gardener were devoted comrades, and spent many an hour pacing solemnly side by side behind the roller or moving machine. But his most constant playmate was the kitten with whom he grew up, and into mature life cat and duck continued their favourite pastime of mock mortal combat, rolling over and over, locked in apparently deadly embrace, a huge delight to both. Humphry's primary mission in life was to clear the garden of snails and slugs, and I have known him eat as many as thirty large snails at a meal, shells and all. The vegetable foods he selected were invariably treasures of the garden. Much had to be forgiven him, and no form of punishment was ever discovered that made the slightest impression on the culprit; he plainly took a droll delight in doing anything he had once clearly understood he was not desired to do. He loved to investigate the house, and would find his way in at an open door and straight to any room where he heard human voices. Visitors grew accustomed to being welcomed in the drawing-room by a vociferous duck, but neighbours were apt to return him with contumely when he was discovered ascending their front stairs.

Letter to *The Spectator*, 18 July 1918

My First Bird

J.A. Baker (1926–1987)

The first bird I searched for was the nightjar, which used
to nest in the valley. Its song is like the sound of a stream
of wine spilling from a height into a deep and booming
cask. It is an odorous sound, with a bouquet that rises to
the quiet sky. In the glare of day it would seem thinner
and drier, but dusk mellows it and gives it vintage. If a
song could smell, this song would smell of crushed grapes
and almonds and dark wood. The sound spills out, and
none of it is lost. The whole wood brims with it. Then it
stops. Suddenly, unexpectedly. But the ear hears it still,
a prolonged and fading echo, draining and winding out
among the surrounding trees. Into the deep stillness,
between the early stars and the long afterglow, the nightjar
leaps up joyfully. It glides and flutters, dances and bounces,
lightly, silently away. In pictures it seems to have a
frog-like despondency, a mournful aura, as though it were
sepulchred in twilight, ghostly and disturbing. It is never
like that in life. Through the dusk, one sees only its shape
and its flight, intangibly light and gay, graceful and nimble
as a swallow.

from *The Peregrine* (1967)

A Tame Rook

Edward Coward (*20th century*)

I had a tame rook many years ago. I picked him up under
the rookery and brought him up by hand. At first he was

housed in a cage, but his wings were never clipped, and as soon as he could fly he took to roosting in a silver birch in the garden. He was called Jack, and would always come or answer when called. There was a rookery near, and the birds would fly round and round the garden calling to him. He would cock his head aside and look up at them, but never showed any disposition to join them. I was farming at the time, and Jack used to accompany me round. He would follow the hoers and haymakers at their work, watching for what might be under the swathe as it was turned over. He would come to the town – a mile and a half away – with me too, flying home when the outskirts were reached. He was a great tease. Nothing pleased him more than to stalk one of the dogs when asleep on the lawn. Jack would give him a vicious dig with his beak, but was much too quick to be caught. He then flew to the lawn gate, where he knew he was safe, and from the top of which he would look down upon the dogs with his head aside and a most whimsical expression on his face, chattering all the time. My mother was fond of gardening, and used to plant out most of her seedlings. Jack would perch on her shoulders and watch her; then when the work was done he would pull them all up. The bird was so fascinating that this was tolerated, but he took to going into the house and pulling the paper off the walls, and so – much to my sorrow – it was decided that Jack must go. He was given to a relative a few miles away, who shut him up in a stable for a few days, but after his release he was never seen again.

Letter to *The Spectator* (*n.d.*)

Fabulous!

Simon Barnes (1951–)

'Fabulous bird,' said Jeremy. It was not the first time I had heard him make such a remark. '*Fabulous, innit?*' Which bird was it? Well, there have been 327 species recorded at Minsmere, so that narrowed things down from the starting point of 10,000-odd species in the entire world. To narrow the field still further, we were in the garden of the Eel's Foot, partaking of the Slimmer's Lunch. The Eel's Foot list is probably quite a long one, and would include Montagu's harrier as well as marsh harrier, but it is safe to assume that it is below 327. The time of year narrows things down still further: the season was settling down, and June was gathering pace fast. Minsmere was consolidating.

'Come on, mate,' Jeremy said. 'Help yourself.' He tossed a chip to the ground, and the fabulous bird hopped up to it, positively swaggering with confidence. It was a rough-looking cockbird, clearly not in the first flush of youth, but a bird boundlessly enthusiastic in the pursuit of life and chips.

'Ah!' I said, smirking at the chance to demonstrate a little newfound erudition. '*Passer domesticus.* Good morning.' The bird gave me a sideways glance and then continued his harassment of the chip. House sparrow. Fabulous.

Jeremy finds all birds fabulous: who am I to disagree? Birds exist for themselves, but that does not mean you are not allowed to enjoy them. Is it horrifically anthropomorphic to enjoy a bird? If so, every ornithologist and every conservationist that ever lived is guilty of this heinous

crime. Birds do not exist so that they can give pleasure
to humanity, but people who fail to delight in a bird are
less than human. Perhaps if you do not permit yourself
to anthropomorphise a little, you are not much of an
anthropos. The more time you are able to spend with birds,
the more they absorb you: not the sudden sights of fabulous
rarities, but the privilege of daily familiarity with their lives.

... And yet one has one's favourites: not because of their
rarity, but perhaps because they seem to express something
of oneself, or one's ideals, one's notions of how life should
be faced. Amid all the fabulousness of Minsmere, there
was *Sterna albifrons*: little tern. They are, in my mind, quite
transcendentally fabulous.

Of all the wild birds of Minsmere, these are the
wildest. They are wild to the point of utter recklessness.
They fling themselves at the surface of the water as if
they had abandoned all thought of self-preservation. They
dive absolutely vertically: a streamlined, winged dagger,
feathered in white and tipped lethally in banana yellow.
There is something magical about all terns; perhaps because
they look so much like seagulls, and yet quite patently are
not. A little tern is what a black-headed gull would look like
in heaven, perhaps: a gull made daintier, faster, sleeker, with
sharper, cleaner lines, and capable of wild, aerial extrava-
gance; a seagull perfected; a seagull angelified.

True, the process of angelification has not reached
the voice. A breeding colony of little terns makes an
appalling racket. Here are some transliterations of their
calls: *krüit-krüit*; *titt-titt*; *tittittittrit-titritt*; *rä-gä-gä-rä-gä-gä*
and *gog-gog*. Perhaps it would be boring if everything sang
like a nightingale. This is just a sample: the little tern has

an enormous range of hideous screams and complicated gobbling noises. The sounds are fabulous enough in their way, but it is in flight that the birds truly express themselves.

They are wonderfully aerobatic. They swerve and cut on wings that slash the air like knives; their ability to change direction is eye-baffling: they can hover with perfect control – and then they perform yet another heart-stopping dive, crashing into the water from twenty feet, always in a perfect vertical. They dive as remorselessly as they do prodigiously: four times as often as a common tern, which is no mean diver itself. And if the common tern dives like a paper aeroplane, the littles dive like little bombs.

… June marched on towards its close, and my next trip to Minsmere brought me plenty of good news: the process of consolidation was continuing. … But it is ever thus in conservation: joy is always mixed with woe. For the little terns at Sizewell had been wiped out. Every single nest had been destroyed.

No, it wasn't some piece of wickedness from the power station people. It was a cockup. Someone had driven onto the beach in a Land Rover … then decided to see *exactly* what the machine could do in four-wheel drive. He chucked it round the beach in great style, and no doubt had a lovely time. Certainly he was utterly ignorant of what he was destroying. And what he destroyed was twenty-nine little tern nests. An entire breeding season was smashed into bits in half-an-hour of fun.

Little terns seem birds born out of their time, but conservationists do what they can to roll time backwards. Conservation is not a Canute-like attempt to resist the tide of progress. It is more a question of facing the future in a sane and sensible fashion. Enough progress has been made at a terrible cost of destruction: further advances now need to be made with a wider vision of what is appropriate: appropriate to mankind and to the world. Conservation is as much progressive as regressive: it is, more than any other viewpoint, concerned with the future, safeguarding it, fighting to make sure that we actually have a future to enjoy. Thus conservationists aim to provide safe nesting sites for a bird that is running out of such places. And in these places, quite incidentally, they give great delight, and that is a wonderful bonus for those who visit them.

Turning the tide of destruction is simply part of the conservationists' daily routine, but they are powerless against sheer bloody idiocy.

from *Flying in the Face of Nature: A Year in Minsmere Bird Reserve* (1992)

A Masked Duck

JONATHAN FRANZEN (1959–)

February 2005, South Texas
At the Santa Ana National Wildlife Refuge, on a hot weekday afternoon, Manley and I hiked several miles down dusty trails to an artificial water feature on the far margin of which I saw three pale-brown ducks. Two of them were paddling with all deliberate speed into the cover of dense reeds, affording me a view mainly of their butts, but the

third bird loitered long enough for me to train my binoculars on its head, which looked as if a person had dipped two fingers in black ink and drawn horizontal lines across its face.

'A masked duck!' I said. 'You see it?'

'I see the duck,' Manley said.

'A masked duck!'

The bird quickly disappeared into the reeds and gave no sign of reemerging. I showed Manley its picture in my *Sibley*.

'I'm not familiar with this duck,' he said. 'But the bird in this picture is the one I just saw.'

'The stripes on its face. The sort of cinnamony brown.'

'Yes.'

'It was a masked duck!'

We were within a few hundred yards of the Rio Grande. On the other side of the river, if you travelled south – say, to Brazil – you could see masked ducks by the dozens. They were a rarity north of the border, though. The pleasure of the sighting sweetened our long tramp back to the parking lot.

While Manley lay down in the car to take a nap, I poked around in a nearby marsh. Three middle-aged white guys with good equipment asked me if I'd seen anything interesting.

'Not much,' I said, 'except a masked duck.'

All three began to talk at once.

'A masked duck!'

'Masked duck?'

'Where exactly? Show us on the map.'

'Are you sure it was a masked duck?'

'You're familiar with the ruddy duck. You do know what a female ruddy looks like.'

'Masked duck!'

I said that, yes, I'd seen female ruddies, we had them in Central Park, and this wasn't a ruddy duck. I said it was as if somebody had dipped two fingers in black ink and –

'Was it alone?'

'Were there others?'

'A masked duck!'

One of the men took out a pen, wrote down my name, and had me pinpoint the location on a map. The other two were already moving down the trail I'd come up.

'And you're sure it was a masked duck,' the third man said.

'It wasn't a ruddy,' I said.

A fourth man stepped out of some bushes right behind us.

'I've got a nighthawk sleeping in a tree.'

'This guy saw a masked duck,' the third man said.

'A masked duck! Are you sure? Are you familiar with the female ruddy?'

The other two men came hurrying back up the trail. 'Did someone say nighthawk?'

'Yeah, I've got a scope on it.'

The five of us went into the bushes. The nighthawk, asleep on a tree branch, looked like a partly balled gray hiking sock. The scope's owner said that the friend of his who'd first spotted the bird had called it a lesser nighthawk, not a common. The well-equipped trio begged to differ.

'He said lesser? Did he hear its call?'

'No,' the man said. 'But the range –'

'Range doesn't help you.'

'Range argues for common, if anything, at this time of year.'

'Look where the wing bar is.'

'Common.'

'Definitely calling it a common.'

The four men set off at a forced-march pace to look for the masked duck, and I began to worry. My identification of the duck, which had felt ironclad in the moment, seemed dangerously hasty in the context of four serious birders marching several miles in the afternoon heat. I went and woke up Manley.

'The only thing that matters,' he said, 'is that we saw it.'

'But the guy took my name down. Now, if they don't see it, I'm going to get a bad rep.'

'If they don't see it, they'll think it's in the reeds.'

'But what if they see ruddies instead? There could be ruddies and masked ducks, and the ruddies aren't as shy.'

'It's something to be anxious about,' Manley said, 'if you want to be anxious about something.'

I went to the refuge visitor center and wrote in the logbook: *One certain and two partially glimpsed* MASKED DUCKS, *north end of Cattail #2.* I asked a volunteer if anyone else had reported a masked duck.

'No, that would be our first this winter,' she said.

from 'My Bird Problem', The New Yorker, 8 August 2005

The Birdwatchers' Dark Grail

HELEN MACDONALD (1970–)

In real life, goshawks resemble sparrowhawks the way leopards resemble housecats. Bigger, yes. But bulkier, bloodier, deadlier, scarier and much, much harder to see. Birds of deep woodland, not gardens, they're the birdwatchers' dark grail. You might spend a week in a forest full of gosses and never see one, just traces of their presence. A sudden hush, followed by the calls of terrified woodland birds, and a sense of something moving just beyond vision. Perhaps you'll find a half-eaten pigeon sprawled in a burst of white feathers on the forest floor. Or you might be lucky: walking in a foggy ride at dawn you'll turn your head and catch a split-second glimpse of a bird hurtling past and away, huge taloned feet held loosely clenched, eyes set on a distant target. A split second that stamps the image indelibly on your brain and leaves you hungry for more. Looking for goshawks is like looking for grace: it comes, but not often, and you don't get to say when or how. But you have a slightly better chance on still, clear mornings in early spring, because that's when goshawks eschew their world under the trees to court each other in the open sky. That was what I was hoping to see. ...

It was eight thirty exactly. I was looking down at a little sprig of mahonia growing out of the turf, its oxblood leaves like buffed pigskin. I glanced up. And then I saw my goshawks. There they were. A pair, soaring above the canopy in the rapidly warming air. There was a flat, hot hand of sun on the back of my neck, but I smelt ice in my nose, seeing those goshawks soaring. I smelt ice and bracken stems and pine resin. Goshawk cocktail. They were on the soar. Goshawks in the air are a complicated grey colour. Not slate grey, nor pigeon grey. But a kind of raincloud grey, and despite their distance, I could see the big powder-puff of white undertail feathers, fanned out, with the thick, blunt tail behind it, and that superb bend and curve of the secondaries of a soaring goshawk that makes them utterly unlike sparrowhawks. And they were being mobbed by crows, and they just didn't care, like, *whatever*. A crow barrelled down on the male and he sort of raised one wing to let the crow past. Crow was not stupid, and didn't dip below the hawk for long. These goshawks weren't fully displaying: there was none of the skydiving I'd read about in books. But they were loving the space between each other, and carving it into all sorts of beautiful concentric chords and distances. A couple of flaps, and the male, the tiercel, would be above the female, and then he'd drift north of her, and then slip down, fast, like a knife-cut, a smooth calligraphic scrawl underneath her, and she'd dip a wing, and then they'd soar up again. They were above a stand of pines, right there. And then they were gone. One minute my pair of goshawks was describing lines from physics textbooks in the sky, and then nothing at all. I don't remember looking down, or away. Perhaps I blinked. Perhaps it was as simple as that. And in that tiny black gap which the brain disguises they'd dived into the wood.

from *H is for Hawk* (2014)

OUTLAND
River, Coast, Sea, Shore

Swans Softly Swimming

Edmund Spenser (1552?–1599)

With that I saw two swans of goodly hue
Come softly swimming down along the Lee;
Two fairer birds I yet did never see;
The snow, which doth the top of Pindus strew,
Did never whiter show,
Nor Jove himself, when he a swan would be
For love of Leda, whiter did appear;
Yet Leda was, they say, as white as he,
Yet not so white as these, nor nothing near;
So purely white they were
That even the gentle stream, the which them bare,
Seemed foul to them, and bade his billows spare
To wet their silken feathers, lest they might
Soil their fair plumes with water not so fair,
And mar their beauties bright,
That shone as heaven's light,
Against their bridal day, which was not long:
　　Sweet Thames, run softly, till I end my song.

from *Prothalamion* (1596)

Lesse then a Goose, and Bigger than a Mallard

SIR FRANCIS DRAKE (1771–1637)

The 24 of *August* being *Bartholomew* day, we fell with 3 Ilands, bearing trianglewise one from another, one of them was very faire and large, and of a fruitfull soile, upon which being next unto us, and the weather very calme, our generall with his gentlemen, and certaine of his mariners, then landed; taking possession thereof in her Maiesties name, and to her use, and called the same *Elizabeth* Iland.

The other two, though they were not so large, nor so faire to the eye, yet were they to us exceeding usefull, for in them we found great store of strange birds, which could not flie at all, nor yet runne so fast, as that they could escape us with their lives: in body they are lesse then a goose, and bigger than a mallard, short and thicke set together, having no feathers, but instead thereof, a certaine hard and matted downe; their beakes are not much unlike the bills of crowes, they lodge and breed upon the land, where making earthes, as the conies doe, in the ground, they lay their egges, and bring up their young; their feeding and provision to live on, is in the sea, where they swimm in such sort, as nature may seeme to have granted them no small prerogative in swiftnesse, both to prey upon others, and themselves to escape from any others that seeke to cease upon them ...

from The World Encompassed by Sir Francis Drake,
Being his next voyage to that to Nombre de Dios formerly imprinted;
carefully collected out of the notes of Master Francis Fletcher preacher
in this imployment, and divers others his followers in the same (1628)

from *The Rime of the Ancient Mariner*

SAMUEL TAYLOR COLERIDGE (1772–1834)

'The ice was here, the ice was there,
The ice was all around:
It cracked and growled, and roared and howled,
Like noises in a swound!

At length did cross an Albatross,
Thorough the fog it came;
As if it had been a Christian soul,
We hailed it in God's name.

It ate the food it ne'er had eat,
And round and round it flew.
The ice did split with a thunder-fit;
The helmsman steered us through!

And a good south wind sprung up behind;
The Albatross did follow,
And every day, for food or play,
Came to the mariners' hollo!

In mist or cloud, on mast or shroud,
It perched for vespers nine;
Whiles all the night, through fog-smoke white,
Glimmered the white Moon-shine.'

'God save thee, ancient Mariner!
From the fiends, that plague thee thus! –
Why look'st thou so?' – With my cross-bow
I shot the ALBATROSS.

Petrels off Three-Hummock Island

Matthew Flinders (1774–1814)

The south-west wind died away in the night; and at six
next morning, Dec. 9, we got under way with a light air
at south-east. After rounding the north-east point of the
three-hummock land, our course westward was pursued
along its north side.

A large flock of gannets was observed at daylight, to
issue out of the great bight to the southward; and they
were followed by such a number of the sooty petrels as we
had never seen equalled. There was a stream of from fifty
to eighty yards in depth, and of three hundred yards, or
more, in breadth; the birds were not scattered, but flying
as compactly as a free movement of their wings seemed
to allow; and during a full *hour and a half*, this stream of
petrels continued to pass without interruption, at a rate
little inferior to the swiftness of the pigeon. On the lowest
computation, I think the number could not have been
less than a hundred millions; and we were thence led to
believe, that there must be, in the large bight, one or more
uninhabited islands of considerable size.

from *A Voyage to Terra Australis* (1814)

Flamborough Head Pilots

WILLIAM FINDEN (1787–1852)

The cliffs, which are of limestone rock, are from three
hundred to four hundred feet high, and their crumbling
sides form the haunt and the breeding place of innumerable
flocks of sea-birds: among which are cormorants, puffins,
razor-bills, and guillemots, with gulls and terns of several
species. Guillemots, which are here extremely numerous,
are known to the seamen of Shields and Newcastle by the
name of 'Flamborough-head pilots', as their presence in
considerable numbers is almost a certain indication of the
ship being 'off the Head'.

from *The Ports, Harbours, Watering-places and
Picturesque Scenery of Great Britain* (1840)

Kingfishers

PERCY BYSSHE SHELLEY (1792–1822)

I cannot tell my joy, when o'er a lake,
Upon a drooping bough with nightshade twined,
I saw two azure halcyons clinging downward
And thinning one bright bunch of amber berries
With quick long beaks, and in the deep there lay
Those lovely forms imaged as in a sky.

from *Prometheus Unbound* (1820)

On the Mud Banks of Northern Patagonia

CHARLES DARWIN (1809–1882)

The ordinary habits of the ostrich are familiar to everyone. They live on vegetable matter, such as roots and grass; but at Bahia Blanca I have repeatedly seen three or four come down at low water to the extensive mud-banks which are then dry, for the sake, as the Gauchos say, of feeding on small fish. Although the ostrich in its habits is so shy, wary, and solitary, and although so fleet in its pace, it is caught without much difficulty by the Indian or Gaucho armed with the bolas. When several horsemen appear in a semi-circle, it becomes confounded, and does not know which way to escape. They generally prefer running against the wind; yet at the first start they expand their wings, and like a vessel make all sail. On one fine hot day I saw several ostriches enter a bed of tall rushes, where they squatted concealed, till quite closely approached. It is not generally known that ostriches readily take to the water. Mr King informs me that at the Bay of San Blas, and at Port Valdes in Patagonia, he saw these birds swimming several times from island to island. They ran into the water both when driven down to a point, and likewise of their own accord when not frightened: the distance crossed was about two hundred yards. When swimming, very little of their bodies appear above water; their necks are extended a little forward, and their progress is slow. On two occasions I saw some ostriches swimming across the Santa Cruz river, where its course was about four hundred yards wide, and the stream rapid.

from *The Voyage of the Beagle* (1845)

Gulls Wailing through the Storm

Philip Henry Gosse (1810–1888)

The shrieking gusts, as the gale rises yet higher and more furious, whip off the crests of the breaking billows, and bear the spray like a shower of salt sleet to the height where we stand; while the foam, as it forms and accumulates around the base of the headland, is seized by the same power in broad masses, and carried against the sides of the projecting rocks; flying hither and thither like fleeces of wool, and adhering like so much mortar to the face of the precipice, till it covers great spaces, to the height of many fathoms above the highest range of the tide. The gulls flit wailing through the storm, now breasting the wind, and beating the air with their long wings as they make slow headway; then, yielding the vain essay, they turn and are whirled away, till, recovering themselves, they come up again with a sweep, only again to be discomfited. Their white forms, now seen against the leaden-grey sky, now lost amidst the snowy foam, then coming into strong relief against the black rocks; their piping screams, now sounding close against the ear, then blending with the sounds of the elements, combine to add a wildness to the scene which was already sufficiently savage.

from *A Year at the Shore* (1865)

Pelicans on the Lagoon

EDWARD LEAR (1812–1888)

29 October 1848
We had soon passed the border of olives that surround
the town, and were trotting over the wide plain, almost
impassable with mud when I had arrived, but now hard
and dry; and beyond this, always making for a little woody
peninsula which projects into the sea, we came to the
salt works. Here they take a sort of mullet, from which
is prepared the roe called 'bottarga,' for which Avlona is
famous. As we skirted these salt lagunes, I observed an
infinite number of what appeared to be large white stones,
arranged in rows with great regularity, though yet with
something odd in their form not easily to be described.
The more I looked at them, the more I felt they were not
what they seemed to be, so I appealed to Blackey, who
instantly plunged into a variety of explanations, verbal and
active; the chief of which consisted in flapping his arms
and hands, puffing and blowing with most uncouth noises,
and putting his head under one arm, with his eyes shut;
as for his language, it was so mixed a jargon of Turkish,
Italian, Greek and Nubian, that little more could be
extracted from it, than that the objects in question ate fish
and flew away afterwards; so I resolved to examine these
mysterious white stones forthwith, and off we went, when
– lo! on my near approach, one and all put forth legs, long
necks, and great wings, and 'stood confessed' so many
great pelicans, which, with croakings expressive of great
disgust at all such ill-timed interruptions, rose up into the

air in a body of five or six hundred, and soared slowly away
to the cliffs north of the gulf.

from Journals of a Landscape Painter in Albania, &c (1851)

By the Chartreuse Torrent

JOHN RUSKIN (1819–1900)

Friday, 4th May. – … I had seen also for the third time, by
the Chartreuse torrent, the most wonderful of all Alpine
birds – a grey, fluttering stealthy creature, about the size
of a sparrow, but of colder grey, and more graceful, which
haunts the sides of the fiercest torrents. There is something
more strange in it than in the seagull – *that* seems a
powerful creature; and the power of the sea, not of a
kind so adverse, so hopelessly destructive; but this small
creature, silent, tender and light, almost like a moth in its
low and irregular flight, – almost touching with its wings
the crests of waves that would overthrow a granite wall,
and haunting the hollows of the black, cold, herbless rocks
that are continually shaken by their spray, has perhaps the
nearest approach to the look of a spiritual existence I know
in animal life.

from Præterita III (1899)

At Bouguizoun Salt Lake in the Sahara

H.B. TRISTRAM (1822–1906)

Not far from this is a small salt lake … which abounds
in birds of every variety. Conspicuous among them is the
flamingo. On approaching the lake a long white line could
be seen stretching right across it looking somewhat by
its slightly undulatory motion like the foam of a line of
breakers on a reef. But the alarm is given: the white line
becomes animated, rises, and expands – first of a snowy
white; then, as the birds simultaneously turn, unfolding
thousands of black wings, it appears a dark speckled
confused mass; then, as they wheel from the spectator,
the soft pink colour of their backs and wing-coverts
absorbs all other hues, and screaming, with outstretched
necks, they fly off, an animated rosy cloud. It is the most
gorgeous sight on which the naturalist's eyes can feast. …
But though the flamingoes have gone on the first alarm,
myriads of birds remain: ducks are swimming literally
'en masse'; clouds of the pretty white-winged black tern
are playing overhead and making feints almost within
reach; while the beautiful black-winged stilt, the tamest
of waders, daintily lifts his long pink legs as he gracefully
stalks through the shallows, or more hurriedly leaves the
nests which are profusely scattered round us, unprotected
and unconcealed among the mud and grass.

The opposite side of the lake is bordered by a mass of
tall reeds, into the recesses of which the water-hens and
purple gallinules are hurrying, and from whose thickets
resounds the harsh note of the great sedge warbler or
thrush nightingale, mingled with the gentler strains

of many lesser aquatic warblers. On all sides of us the
collared pratincole is exercising its arts, like the lapwing,
to lure us from the eggs which lie scattered on the hard
dried mud, dropped by threes into any chance camel's
footmark; and groups of little Kentish plover are running
rapidly by the water's edge.

from *The Great Sahara: Wanderings South of the Atlas Mountains* (1860)

Herald Island Nurseries

JOHN MUIR (1838–1914)

Herald Island, July 31, 1881
Innumerable gulls and murres breed on the steep cliffs,
the latter most abundant. They kept up a constant din of
domestic notes. Some of them are sitting on their eggs,
others have young, and it seems astonishing that either
eggs or the young can find a resting-place on cliffs so
severely precipitous. The nurseries formed a lively picture
– the parents coming and going with food or to seek it,
thousands in rows standing on narrow ledges like bottles
on a grocer's shelves, the feeding of the little ones, the
multitude of wings, etc.

from *The Cruise of the Corwin* (1917)

from *The Penguins' Rock*

GUY DE MAUPASSANT (1850–1893)

The penguin is a very rare bird of passage, with peculiar habits. It lives the greater part of the year in the latitude of Newfoundland and the islands of St. Pierre and Miquelon. But in the breeding season a flight of emigrants crosses the ocean and comes every year to the same spot to lay their eggs, to the Penguins' Rock near Etretat. They are found nowhere else, only there. They have always come there, have always been chased away, but return again, and will always return. As soon as the young birds are grown they all fly away, and disappear for a year.

Why do they not go elsewhere? Why not choose some other spot on the long white, unending cliff that extends from the Pas-de-Calais to Havre? What force, what invincible instinct, what custom of centuries impels these birds to come back to this place? What first migration, what tempest, possibly, once cast their ancestors on this rock? And why do the children, the grandchildren, all the descendants of the first parents always return here?

There are not many of them, a hundred at most, as if one single family, maintaining the tradition, made this annual pilgrimage.

And each spring, as soon as the little wandering tribe has taken up its abode an the rock, the same sportsmen also reappear in the village. One knew them formerly when they were young; now they are old, but constant to the regular appointment which they have kept for thirty or forty years. They would not miss it for anything in the world.

Flamingo City

ABEL CHAPMAN (1851–1929) & WALTER J. BUCK (*n.d.*)

May 9 [*1883*] – The immense aggregations of flamingoes which, in wet seasons, throng the middle marismas can scarce be described. Our bird-islets lay so remote from the low-lying shores that no land whatever was in sight; but the desolate horizon that surrounded them was adorned by an almost unbroken line of pink and white that separated sea and sky over the greater part of the circle. ...

On approach, the cause of the peculiar appearance of the flamingo city from a distance became clearly discernible. Hundreds of birds were sitting down on a low mud-island, hundreds more were standing erect thereon, while others stood in the water alongside. Thus the different elevations of their bodies formed what had appeared a triple or quadruple line.

On reaching the spot, we found a perfect mass of nests. The low, flat mud-plateau was crowded with them as thickly as its space permitted. The nests had little or no height above the dead-level mud – some were raised an inch or two, a few might reach four or five inches in height, but the majority were merely circular bulwarks of mud barely raised above the general level, and bearing the impression of the bird's legs distinctly marked upon the periphery. The general aspect of the plateau might be likened to a large table covered with plates. In the centre was a deep hole full of muddy water, which, from the gouged appearance of its sides, had probably supplied the birds with building material.

from *Unexplored Spain*

Courting Shags

EDMUND SELOUS (1857–1934)

Either at once from where he stands, or after first
waddling a step or two, he makes an impressive jump or
hop towards her, and stretching his long neck straight up,
or even a little backwards, he at the same time throws
back his head so that it is in one line with it, and opens his
beak rather widely. In a second or so he closes it, and then
he opens and shuts it again several times in succession,
rather more quickly. Then he sinks forward with his breast
on the rock, so that he lies all along it, and fanning out his
small, stiff tail, bends it over his back whilst at the same
time stretching his head and neck backwards towards it,
till with his beak he sometimes seizes and, apparently,
plays with the feathers. In this attitude he may remain for
some seconds more or less, having all the while a languishing or ecstatic expression, after which he brings his head
forward again, and then repeats the performance some
three or four or, perhaps, half-a-dozen times. This would
seem to be the full courting display, the complete figure
so to speak, but it is not always fully gone through. It may
be acted part at a time. The first part, commencing with
the hop – the *simple aveu* as it may be called – is not always
followed by the ecstasy in the recumbent posture, and the
last is still more often indulged in without this preliminary,
whilst the bird is sitting thus upon the rock. Again, a bird
whilst standing, but not quite erect, will dart his head
forward and upward, and make with his bill as though
snapping at insects in the air. Then, after a second or
two, he will throw his head back till it touches or almost

touches the centre of his back, and whilst at the same time opening and shutting the beak, communicate a quick vibratory motion to the throat. It looks as though he were executing a trill or doing the *tremulo* so loved of Italian singers, of which, however, there is no vocal evidence.

When the male bird makes the great pompous hop up to the female, and then, after the preliminaries that I have described, falls prone in front of her, he is, so to speak, at her feet; but by throwing his head backwards he gets practically farther off, nor can he well see her whilst staring up into the sky behind him, which is what he appears to be doing. Thus the first warmth of the situation is a little chilled, and on the stage we should call it an uncomfortable distance. The female shag seems to think so too, for all that she does – that is to say, all that I have then seen her do – is to stand and look about, conduct which, as it is uninteresting, we may perhaps assume to be correct. But when the antics begin, as one may say, from the second figure, the male not rising from his recumbent position (a quite usual one) on the rock to make the first display, the bird towards whom his attentions are directed will often be standing behind him, and it then appears as if he had brought back his head in order to gaze up at her *con expressione*. In this case she, on her part, will sometimes cosset the feathers of his throat or neck with the tip of her hooked bill, a courtesy which you see him acknowledge by sundry little pleased movings of his head to one side and to another.

from *Bird-Watching* (1901)

Ducks' Ditty

KENNETH GRAHAME (1859–1932)

All along the backwater,
Through the rushes tall,
Ducks are a-dabbling,
Up tails all!

Ducks' tails, drakes' tails,
Yellow feet a-quiver,
Yellow bills all out of sight
Busy in the river!

Slushy green undergrowth
Where the roach swim –
Here we keep our larder,
Cool and full and dim.

Everyone for what he likes!
We like to be
Heads down, tails up,
Dabbling free!

High in the blue above
Swifts whirl and call –
We are down a-dabbling
Up tails all!

from *The Wind in the Willows* (1908)

The Kingfisher

W.H. DAVIES (1871–1940)

It was the Rainbow gave thee birth,
   And left thee all her lovely hues;
And, as her mother's name was Tears,
   So runs it in thy blood to choose
For haunts the lonely pools, and keep
In company with trees that weep.

Go you and, with such glorious hues,
   Live with proud Peacocks in green parks;
On lawns as smooth as shining glass,
   Let every feather show its marks;
Get thee on boughs and clap thy wings
Before the windows of proud kings.

Nay, lovely Bird, thou art not vain;
   Thou hast no proud ambitious mind;
I also love a quiet place
   That's green, away from all mankind;
A lonely pool, and let a tree
Sigh with her bosom over me.

The Watering-Place

Jacques Delamain (1874–1953)

In an indentation of the bank, on a gentle slope,
extends a little exposed strand, the watering-place,
a vital spot, that to its faithful seems surrounded
by a bit of mystery. All the birds of the region
know it, but rarely approach it then and there, as
if they feel that in the short moment when they are
settled on the bare earth, without the protection
of leaves or grasses, they are exposing themselves
to unusual perils. The brighter the dress of the
visitor, the more guarded his approach. An Oriole
whistles for a long time among the poplars before
resolving to descend toward that liquid mirror
which, reflecting his beauty, is to render him still
more conspicuous. A Green Woodpecker, a Great
Spotted Woodpecker, mottled in black and white,
clutch the trunks of three or four adjoining trees
in succession, each time a little lower down, before
arriving at the water, as if by dangerous rungs. A
male Linnet whose breast has already lost the bright
carmine of his springtime livery, is on the watch,
perched on a thistle very near by. He hesitates, then
settles on the ground. Eye attentive, body alert, he
touches the liquid with his bill, raises his head and,
straightening his stretched-out neck, savours the cool
sip. The gesture is repeated several times, then the
bird withdraws. In almost every species, the rite is
the same. However, the Ringdoves and Turtledoves
plunge their whole bills into the water which they

suck in one gulp with pulsations of their throats. Others, like the Swallows and Swifts, slow down their flight a little to drink, skim over the still surface, touch it with their mandibles, and break it into a thousand little ripples.

from *Why Birds Sing* (1932)

Birds on the Flats

RACHEL CARSON (1907–1964)

The flats took on a mysterious quality as dusk approached
and the last evening light was reflected from the scattered
pools and creeks. Then birds became only dark shadows,
with no color discernible. Sanderlings scurried across the
beach like little ghosts, and here and there the darker
forms of the willets stood out. Often I could come very
close to them before they would start up in alarm – the
sanderlings running, the willets flying up, crying. Black
skimmers flew along the ocean's edge silhouetted against
the dull, metallic gleam, or they went flitting above
the sand like large, dimly seen moths. Sometimes they
'skimmed' the winding creeks of tidal water, where little
spreading surface ripples marked the presence of small fish.

from *The Edge of the Sea* (1955)

A Black Cloud of Pinkfooted Geese

SIR PETER SCOTT (1909–1989)

All day we had watched them straggling in in bunches of half a dozen to a dozen – tiny specks in the sky suddenly hurtling downward to settle on the marsh. They had done it all the day before, and the day before that too – arriving from Spitzbergen and Iceland and Greenland.

Some of them flew out and settled on the sand, and we tried to estimate their numbers. We counted and multiplied, counted and multiplied, starting first at one end and then at the other. Eight thousand was our estimate after half an hour of eye-straining through a field glass.

And then suddenly behind us a roar broke out, and the whole surface of the marsh seemed to rise into the air. A black cloud of geese, which conveyed just the same oppressiveness as an approaching rain-storm, moved out over the sand where sat the ones we had been counting. They did not settle with them, however, but stretched away down the crest of the high sand until those that pitched farthest were only visible as they turned to head the wind; fully two miles of solid pinkfooted geese. …

Is it possible that 20,000 geese made up that black line which stretched as far as the eye could reach along the high sand?

Perhaps there were half of the pinkfooted geese that exist in the world here before us.

from *Morning Flight* (1935)

The Dipper
KATHLEEN JAMIE (1962–)

It was winter, near freezing,
I'd walked through a forest of firs
when I saw issue out of the waterfall
a solitary bird.

It lit on a damp rock,
and, as water swept stupidly on,
wrung from its own throat
supple, undammable song.

It isn't mine to give.
I can't coax this bird to my hand
that knows the depth of the river
yet sings of it on land.

A BIRDING YEAR
Winter

Then Nightly Sings the Staring Owl

WILLIAM SHAKESPEARE (1564–1616)

When icicles hang by the wall,
   And Dick the shepherd blows his nail,
And Tom bears logs into the hall,
   And milk comes frozen home in pail;
When blood is nipped, and ways be foul,
Then nightly sings the staring owl:
Tu-whit, tu-whoo – a merry note,
While greasy Joan doth keel the pot.

When all aloud the wind doth blow,
   And coughing drowns the parson's saw,
And birds sit brooding in the snow,
   And Marian's nose looks red and raw;
When roasted crabs hiss in the bowl,
Then nightly sings the staring owl:
Tu-whit, tu-whoo – a merry note,
While greasy Joan doth keel the pot.

from *Love's Labour's Lost*

Titmouse Winters

GILBERT WHITE (1720–1793)

Every species of titmouse winters with us; they have
what I call a kind of intermediate bill between the hard
and the soft, between the Linnaean genera of *Fringilla*
and *Motacilla*. One species alone spends its whole time in
the woods and fields, never retreating for succour in the

severest seasons to houses and neighbourhoods; and that is the delicate long-tailed titmouse, which is almost as minute as the golden-crowned wren: but the blue titmouse, or nun (*Parus caeruleus*), the cole-mouse (*Parus ater*), the great black-headed titmouse (*Fringillago*), and the marsh titmouse (*Parus palustris*), all resort, at times, to buildings; and in hard weather particularly. The great titmouse, driven by stress of weather, much frequents houses, and, in deep snows, I have seen this bird, while it hung with its back downwards (to my no small delight and admiration), draw straw lengthwise from out the eaves of thatched houses, in order to pull out the flies that were concealed between them, and that in such numbers that they quite defaced the thatch, and gave it a ragged appearance.

The blue titmouse, or nun, is a great frequenter of houses, and a general devourer. Beside insects, it is very fond of flesh; for it frequently picks bones on dung-hills: it is a vast admirer of suet, and haunts butchers' shops. When a boy, I have known twenty in a morning caught with snap mousetraps, baited with tallow or suet. It will also pick holes in apples left on the ground, and be well entertained with the seeds on the head of a sunflower. The blue, marsh, and great titmice will, in very severe weather, carry away barley and oat straws from the sides of ricks.

from Letter to Thomas Pennant, Esquire,
in *The Natural History of Selborne* (1789)

A Winter Visitor, the Wren

Susan Fenimore Cooper (1813–1894)

He is a very great builder, also, is the wren. He seems
to think, like that famous old Countess of yore, Bess of
Shrewsbury, that he is doomed to build for his life. Frequently while his mate is sitting, he will build you several
useless nests, just for his own gratification; singing away all
the time, and telling his more patient mate, perhaps, what
straws he picks up, and where he finds them. Sometimes,
when he first arrives, if not already mated, he will build
his house, and then look out for a wife afterwards. It is a
pity they should not stay with us all winter, these pleasant
little friends of ours, like the European wren, who never
migrates, and sings all the year round. It is true, among
the half dozen varieties which visit us, there is the winter
wren, who remains during the cold weather in some parts
of the State; but we do not see him here after the snow has
fallen, and at best he appears much less musical than the
summer bird. Our common house-wren is a finer singer
than the European bird; but he flies far to the southward,
in winter, and sings Spanish in Mexico and South America.

from *Rural Hours* (1887)

The Little Brown Birds
CHARLOTTE BRONTË (1816–1855)

It was three o'clock; the church bell tolled as I passed
under the belfry: the charm of the hour lay in its approaching dimness, in the low-gliding and pale-beaming sun. I
was a mile from Thornfield, in a lane noted for wild roses
in summer, for nuts and blackberries in autumn, and even
now possessing a few coral treasures in hips and haws,
but whose best winter delight lay in its utter solitude and
leafless repose. If a breath of air stirred, it made no sound
here; for there was not a holly, not an evergreen to rustle,
and the stripped hawthorn and hazel bushes were as still
as the white, worn stones which causewayed the middle
of the path. Far and wide, on each side, there were only
fields, where no cattle now browsed; and the little brown
birds, which stirred occasionally in the hedge, looked like
single russet leaves that had forgotten to drop.

from *Jane Eyre* (1847)

An Owl in Winter Woods
HENRY DAVID THOREAU (1817–1862)

In the deepest snows, the path which I used from the
highway to my house, about half a mile long, might have
been represented by a meandering dotted line, with wide
intervals between the dots. For a week of even weather I
took exactly the same number of steps, and of the same
length, coming and going, stepping deliberately and with
the precision of a pair of dividers in my own deep tracks,

– to such routine the winter reduces us, – yet often they were filled with heaven's own blue. … One afternoon I amused myself by watching a barred owl … sitting on one of the lower dead limbs of a white-pine, close to the trunk, in broad daylight, I standing within a rod of him. He could hear me when I moved and crunched the snow with my feet, but could not plainly see me. When I made most noise he would stretch out his neck, and erect his neck feathers, and open his eyes wide; but their lids soon fell again, and he began to nod. I too felt a slumberous influence after watching him half an hour, as he sat thus with his eyes half-open, like a cat, winged brother of the cat. There was only a narrow slit left between their lids, by which he preserved a peninsular relation to me; thus, with half-shut eyes, looking out from the land of dreams, and endeavouring to realise me, vague object or mote that interrupted his visions. At length, on some louder noise or my nearer approach, he would grow uneasy and sluggishly turn about on his perch, as if impatient at having his dreams disturbed; and when he launched himself off and flapped through the pines, spreading his wings to unexpected breadth, I could not hear the slightest sound from them. Thus, guided amid the pine boughs rather by a delicate sense of their neighbourhood than by sight, feeling his twilight way as it were with his sensitive pinions, he found a new perch, where he might in peace await the dawning of his day.

from *Walden or Life in the Woods* (1927)

I Hear the Woodpeckers Knocking

CHARLES ELIOT NORTON (1827–1908)

To John Ruskin, from Shady Hill, April 9th, 1887.
The winter has been long and hard with us. Even yet there are snowbanks in shady places, and not yet is there a sign of a leaf. Even the snowdrops are hardly venturing out of the earth. But the birds have come back, and to-day I hear the woodpeckers knocking at the doors of the old trees to find a shelter and home for the summer.

from John Ruskin, *Præterita III* (1899)

Partridge in the Snow

JOHN BURROUGHS (1837–1921)

The partridge (*Bonasa umbellus*) is one of our most native and characteristic birds. The woods seem good to be in where I find him. He gives a habitable air to the forest, and one feels as if the rightful occupant was really at home. The woods where I do not find him seem to want something, as if suffering from some neglect of Nature. And then he is such a splendid success, so hardy and vigorous. I think he enjoys the cold and the snow. His wings seem to rustle with more fervency in midwinter. If the snow falls very fast, and promises a heavy storm, he will complacently sit down and allow himself to be snowed under. Approaching him at such times, he suddenly bursts out of the snow at your feet, scattering the flakes in all directions, and goes humming away through the woods like a bombshell, – a picture of native spirit and success.

from *Wake-Robin* (1917)

Yosemite in Winter

JOHN MUIR (1838–1914)

The short, cold days of winter are also sweetened with
the music and hopeful chatter of a considerable number
of birds. No cheerier choir ever sang in snow. First and
best of all is the water-ouzel, a dainty, dusky little bird
about the size of a robin, that sings in sweet fluty song all
winter and all summer, in storms and calms, sunshine and
shadow, haunting the rapids and waterfalls with marvellous
constancy, building his nest in the cleft of a rock bathed
in spray. He is not web-footed, yet he dives fearlessly into
foaming rapids, seeming to take the greater delight the
more boisterous the stream, always as cheerful and calm as
any linnet in a grove. All his gestures as he flits about amid
the loud uproar of the falls bespeak the utmost simplicity
and confidence – bird and stream one and inseparable.
What a pair! yet they are well related. A finer bloom than
the foam bell in an eddying pool is this little bird. We may
miss the meaning of the loud-resounding torrent, but the
flute-like voice of the bird – only love is in it.

from *The Yosemite* (1912)

The Crows at Washington

JOHN HAY (1838–1905)

Slow flapping to the setting sun
    By twos and threes in wavering rows.
    As twilight shadows dimly close,
The crows fly over Washington.

Under the crimson sunset sky
Virginian woodlands leafless lie,
    In wintry torpor bleak and dun.
Through the rich vault of heaven, which shines
    Like a warmed opal in the sun,
With wide advance in broken lines
    The crows fly over Washington.

Over the Capitol's white dome,
    Across the obelisk soaring bare
To prick the clouds, they travel home,
Content and weary, winnowing
    With dusky vans the golden air,
Which hints the coming of the spring,
    Though winter whitens Washington.

The dim, deep air, the level ray
Of dying sunlight on their plumes,
    Give them a beauty not their own;
Their hoarse notes fail and faint away;
    A rustling murmur floating down
Blends sweetly with the thickening glooms;

They touch with grace the fading day,
  Slow flying over Washington.

I stand and watch with clouded eyes
  These dim battalions move along;
Out of the distance memory cries
  Of days when life and hope were strong,
When love was prompt and wit was gay;
Even then, at evening, as to-day,
  I watched, while twilight hovered dim
  Over Potomac's curving rim,
This selfsame flight of homing crows
Blotting the sunset's fading rose
  Above the roofs of Washington.

The Darkling Thrush

THOMAS HARDY (1840–1928)

I leant upon a coppice gate
  When Frost was spectre-grey,
And Winter's dregs made desolate
  The weakening eye of day.
The tangled bine-stems scored the sky
  Like strings from broken lyres,
And all mankind that haunted nigh
  Had sought their household fires.

The land's sharp features seemed to be
    The Century's corpse outleant,
His crypt the cloudy canopy,
    The wind his death-lament.
The ancient pulse of germ and birth
    Was shrunken hard and dry,
And every spirit upon earth
    Seemed fervourless as I.

At once a voice burst forth among
    The bleak twigs overhead
In a full-hearted evensong
    Of joy illimited;
An agèd thrush, frail, gaunt, and small,
    In blast-beruffled plume,
Had chosen thus to fling his soul
    Upon the growing gloom.

So little cause for carolings
    Of such ecstatic sound
Was written on terrestrial things
    Afar or nigh around,
That I could think there trembled through
    His happy good-night air
Some blessed Hope, whereof he knew
    And I was unaware.

The Irresolute Meadow Pipit

W.H. HUDSON (1841–1922)

He did not sing, even on those bright days or hours in
January, which caused such silent ones as the corn bunting
and pied wagtail to break out in melody. The bell-like
tinkling strain he utters when soaring up and dropping to
earth is for summer only: it is that faint fairy-like aerial
music which you hear on wide moors and commons and
lonely hillsides. In winter he has no language but that one
sharp sorrowful little call, or complaint, the most anxious
sound uttered by any small bird in these islands. It is a
sound that suits the place, and when the wind blows hard,
bringing the noise of the waves to your ears, and the salt
spray; when all the sky is one grey cloud, and sea mists
sweep over the earth at intervals blurring the outline of
the hills, that thin but penetrative little sad call seems
more appropriate than ever and in tune with Nature and
the mind. The movements, too, of the unhappy little
creature have a share in the impression he makes; he flings
himself up, as it were, before your footsteps out of the
brown heath, pale tall grasses and old dead bracken, and
goes off as if blown away by the wind, then returns to you
as if blown back, and hovers and goes to this side, then
to that, now close to you, a little sombre bird, and anon
in appearance a mere dead leaf or feather whirled away
before the blast. During the uncertain flight, and when, at
intervals, he drops upon a rock close by, he continues to
emit the sharp sorrowful note, and if you listen it infects
your mind with its sadness and mystery.

from *The Land's End: A Naturalist's Impressions in West Cornwall* (1908)

Cranes

EKAI KAWAGUCHI (1866–1945)

I almost trembled at a prospect of spending another perilous night in the snow. Just at that juncture I heard some clear, ringing sounds, as of a bird's cry. Turning round, I saw seven or eight cranes stalking along majestically in the shallow part of the river. Never before had I seen a sight so poetically picturesque, so representative of antique serenity. Some little time afterwards I composed an *uta* in memory of that enchanting scene:

> Like feathers white the snows fall down and lie
> > There on the mountain-river's sandy banks;
> Ko-kow, Ko-kow! sounds strange – a melody
> > I hear – I search around for this strange cry.
> In quiet majesty those mountain cranes
> > I find, are proudly strutting – singing thus.

from *Three Years in Tibet* (1909)

The Yellow Bunting Claims its Territory

H. Eliot Howard (1873–1940)

Under normal conditions the ordinary winter routine
continues until early in February; but the male then
deserts the flock, seeks a position of its own, and becomes
isolated from its companions. Now the position which it
selects does not, as a rule, embrace a very large area – a
few acres perhaps at the most. But there is always some
one point which is singled out and resorted to with marked
frequency – a tree, a bush, a gate-post, a railing, anything
in fact which can form a convenient perch, and eventually
it becomes a central part of the bird's environment. Here
it spends the greater part of its time, here it utters its song
persistently, and here it keeps watch upon intruders. The
process of establishment is nevertheless a gradual one. The
male does not appear in its few acres suddenly and remain
there permanently as does the migrant; at first it may
not even roost in the prospective territory. The course of
procedure is somewhat as follows:– At dawn it arrives and
for a while utters its song, preens its feathers, or searches
for food; then it vanishes, rising into the air and flying
in one fixed direction as far as the eye can follow, until
it becomes a speck upon the horizon and is ultimately
lost to view. During these excursions it rejoins the small
composite flocks which still frequent the fields and farm
buildings. For a time the hedgerow is deserted and the
bird remains with its companions. But one does not have
to wait long for the return; it reappears as suddenly as
it vanished, flying straight back to the few acres which
constitute its territory, back even to the same gate-post

or railing, where it again sings. This simple routine may be repeated quite a number of times during the first two hours or so of daylight, with, of course, a certain amount of variation; on one occasion the bird may be away for a few minutes only, on another for perhaps half an hour, whilst sometimes it will fly for a few hundred yards, hesitate, and then return – all of which shows clearly enough that these few acres possess some peculiar signifi-cance and are capable of exercising a powerful influence upon the course of its behaviour. And so the disposition in relation to the territory becomes dominant in the life of the bird.

from *Territory in Bird Life* (1920)

Winter Chorus

Jacques Delamain (1874–1953)

November morning. The bird choruses begin with a soft whispering. On the edge of the wood, in the peat-bog, where trails of mist still linger above over-flowing ditches, a flock of green Siskins arrived a few days ago from the forests of the north, burst forth from the alders with a crackling of metallic notes. More distant, in the sheltered valley, a band of Starlings fills the top of a poplar with a gossiping sung, spoken, and whistled, all at once, composed of all the sounds of nature, which these mimics in black coats dotted with white have picked up in their comings and goings between the plain and the forest. A dozen little Serins, green like the Siskins, but tinier and with shorter bills, send filtering through the needles of the sea-pines a thread of thin strident sound like the rustling noise of grasshoppers. On the sunny slope of the limestone hillock a ringing like the knocking together of glass beads identifies in the walnut tree a flock of Corn Buntings motionless as the brown leaves that winter has probably forgotten on their branches. A little later, with the last burnished rays of light, another chorus, clearest and freshest of all perhaps, the Linnets, will cheer up the dying day.

from Why Birds Sing (1932)

Winter
EDWARD THOMAS (1878–1917)

Dec. 21
Larks and sparrows unite their flocks.
   Thrushes sing short broken melodies.
   Bullfinches and wrens singly in the frost. ...
   Loud shuffling of the blackbirds in the undergrowth. ...
   Pheasants roosting at night, very conspicuous on the bare boughs; sleep heavily and do not readily quit their perches.

Dec. 28
Wheatears linger singly in the gorse.

from The Woodland Life (1897)

from *The Blue Jay*

D.H. LAWRENCE (1885–1930)

The blue jay with a crest on his head
Comes round the cabin in the snow.
He runs in the snow like a bit of blue metal
Turning his back on everything.

From the pine-tree that towers and hisses like a pillar of
    shaggy smoke
Immense above the cabin
Comes a strident laugh as we approach, this little black dog
    and I;
So halts the little black bitch on four spread paws in the snow
And looks up inquiringly into the pillar of cloud,
With a tinge of misgiving.
Ca-a-a! comes the scrape of ridicule out of the tree.
  ...
Every day since the snow is here
The blue jay paces round the cabin, very busy, picking up bits,
Turning his back on us all,
And bobbing his thick dark crest about the snow, as if darkly
    saying:
I ignore those folk who look out.

You acid blue metallic bird,
You thick bird with a strong crest
Who are you?
Whose boss are you, with all your bully way?
You copper-sulphate blue bird!

The Goldcrest's Winter

Stephen Moss (1960–)

As I walk past the churchyard, I hear a distinctive sound
coming from the dense, dark foliage of the yew trees.
A high-pitched, rhythmic snatch of birdsong, almost
childlike in its tone and pattern – 'diddly-diddly-diddly-
diddly-deeee'. This is the sound of the smallest bird
in the parish, and indeed the smallest in Britain: the
goldcrest. Tiny, plump, and decked in pastel shades of
green, the goldcrest can sometimes be glimpsed as it flits
around the outer foliage of the yews, before plunging
back into the dark interior.

This creature is a true featherweight, tipping the
scales at just one-fifth of an ounce: about the same as a
twenty-pence coin, or a single sheet of A4 paper. Small
size is bad news if you want to survive during long spells
of cold weather. The smaller you are, the higher your
ratio of surface area to volume; which means that a bird
the size of a goldcrest loses heat very rapidly indeed. So
like other small birds, it must feed constantly through
the short winter days, to get enough energy to keep it
alive through the long, cold nights.

Most insect-eating birds don't even try to survive
the British winter; instead they head south to warmer
climes, where food is easier to find. But the goldcrest
has a secret weapon: its association with evergreens
such as the yew. Because these trees don't shed
their leaves in winter, their dense foliage is home to
thousands of tiny insects. The goldcrest is the only
bird small enough to survive on these minuscule

creatures, and will spend the coldest months of the year inside our churchyard yews; feeding by day, and huddled up for warmth by night.

On bright, sunny days, even in the middle of winter, I occasionally see the male goldcrest puffing up his chest, momentarily flashing his golden crown like a shaft of sunlight piercing through a winter sky, and issuing a burst of song. It is a curiously optimistic sound for this time of year, and a reminder that however cold the weather may still be, spring will eventually arrive.

from *Wild Hares and Hummingbirds:*
The Natural History of an English Village (2012)

Willow Warbler

SÍOFRA MCSHERRY (1983–)

A night migrant, the willow warbler
is believed to navigate by the stars,
although this cannot be proved.
Winter weathering in West Africa,
twice a year he quarters the globe
with the handspan of himself,
to wash his wings in the hot sand,
chasing summer, chasing light.

He leaves us with winter,
which is just as true as summer
but empty of warblers.
We are left with the cold truth of it,
the freezing, the shutting down,
the narrowing, and the wait.

2011

INDEX *of* AUTHORS

INDEX *of* BIRDS

INDEX *of* ILLUSTRATIONS

ACKNOWLEDGEMENTS

Thanks are due to the following for their kind permission to include material in this book:
'The Buzzards' from *The Buzzards and Other Poems* by Martin Armstrong reprinted by permission
of Peters Fraser & Dunlop (www.petersfraserdunlop.com) on behalf of the Estate of Martin
Armstrong. Excerpt from *The Peregrine* reprinted by permission of HarperCollins Publishers
Ltd © J.A. Baker 1967. Edouard Bamporiki, 'A Cock Crows in Rwanda' translated by Arlette
Maregeya & David Shook from *The World Record: International Voices from Southbank Centre's Poetry
Parnassus*, Bloodaxe, 2012, edited by Neil Astley and Anna Selby. Reproduced by permission of
David Shook. Excerpt from Simon Barnes, *Flying in the Face of Nature: A Year in Minsmere Bird Reserve*
(Pelham Books, 1992) © Simon Barnes 1992. Reproduced by permission of Simon Barnes c/o
Georgina Capel Associates Ltd, 29 Wardour Street, London, w1d 6ps. Excerpt from *The Edge of
the Sea* by Rachel Carson, © 1955 by Rachel L. Carson. Reprinted by permission. Excerpt from
'The Mountain of Birds' from *Ottoman Explorations of the Nile: Evliya Çelebi's 'Matchless Pearl These
Reports of the Nile' map and his accounts of the Nile and the Horn of Africa in The Book of Travels*, Part
II: *Third Journey: Cairo–Luxor–Ibrim*, ed. Robert Dankoff, Nuran Tezcan & Michael D. Sheridan,
2018, reprinted by permission of Gingko Library. The Agreed Upon 215 words from *At the Source*
by Gillian Clarke. Published by Carcanet, 2008. © Gillian Clarke. Reproduced by permission of
the author c/o Rogers, Coleridge & White Ltd, 20 Powis Mews, London w11 1jn. Excerpt from
The Running Sky: A Birdwatching Life © Tim Dee (Jonathan Cape, 2009) reproduced by permission
of Tim Dee/United Agents. Excerpt from *Pourquoi les oiseaux chantent* by Jacques Delamain ©
Editions Stock 1928. 'My Bird Problem' © 2005 by Jonathan Franzen originally appeared in
The New Yorker. Reprinted by permission of Writers House llc acting as agent for the author.
(Excerpt). The Agreed Upon 183 Words from *At Hawthorn Time* by Melissa Harrison. Published
by Bloomsbury, 2015. © Melissa Harrison. Reproduced by permission of the author c/o Rogers,
Coleridge & White Ltd, 20 Powis Mews, London w11 1jn. Excerpt from *A Kestrel for a Knave* by
Barry Hines reproduced by permission of The Agency (London) Ltd © Barry Hines, 1968. All
rights reserved and enquiries to The Agency (London) Ltd, 24 Pottery Lane, London w11 4lz.
'Hawk Roosting' from *Lupercal* © Ted Hughes, Faber & Faber, 1960, reproduced by permission
of Faber & Faber. 'The Dipper' from *The Tree House* (Picador, 2004) and excerpt from *Sightlines*
(Sort Of Books, 2012) by Kathleen Jamie reproduced by permission of the author. Excerpt from
Kingbird Highway: The Story of a Natural Obsession that Got a Little Out of Hand by Kenn Kaufman.
© 1997 by Kenn Kaufman. Reprinted by permission of Houghton Mifflin Harcourt Publishing
Company. All rights reserved. Excerpt of 442 words from *Prodigal Summer* by Barbara Kingsolver.
© 2000 by Barbara Kingsolver. Reprinted by permission of HarperCollins Publishers and The
Frances Goldin Literary Agency. 'Greenshank' © the estate of Norman MacCaig. Reproduced
from *The Poems of Norman MacCaig*, edited by Ewen MacCaig, Polygon, 2009, with the permission
of the Licensor through PLSclear. Excerpts from *H is for Hawk* © 2014 by Helen Macdonald.
'Willow Warbler' by Síofra McSherry reproduced by permission of the author. Excerpt from
Some Birds of the Countryside: The Art of Nature reprinted by permission of The Society of Authors
as the Literary Representative for the Estate of H.J. Massingham. Excerpt from *Wild Hares and
Hummingbirds: The Natural History of an English Village* by Stephen Moss (Vintage, 2012) reprinted by
permission of Vintage/Penguin Random House. 'A Fleet of Eagles' from *Limits VIII* (1964–66) by
Christopher Okigbo, reprinted by permission of The Christopher Okigbo Foundation. 'Summer
for an Instant' by George Orwell (© George Orwell 1933). Reprinted by kind permission of Bill
Hamilton as the Literary Executor of the Estate of Sonia Brownell. Excerpt from 'The Migration',
Granta 102: The New Nature Writing: Essays & Memoir (2008) © Edward Platt, reproduced by kind
permission of Edward Platt/United Agents. Excerpt from *Morning Flight* by Sir Peter Scott
(Charles Scribner's Sons, 1935) reproduced by permission of Dafila Scott. 'Mallard' by Rex
Warner reproduced with permission from Curtis Brown Group Ltd on behalf of the beneficiaries
of The Estate of Rex Warner. © Rex Warner 1937. Excerpt from T.H. White, *The Once and Future
King*, HarperCollins, 1958 reproduced by permission of David Higham Associates. Excerpt from
The Lone Swallows (Collins, 1922) by Henry Williamson © HW Literary Estate.